WHAT IF

Other books by Hydee Tehana

Fire and Water: Awakening the Dragon Within

What If…Death is a Doorway?

What If…Belief Systems Are Just BS?

WHAT IF…

WE ARE INTERGALACTIC INTELLIGENCE?

by

Hydee Tehana

Trinity Rose Productions, LLC
Kealakekua, Hawaii

WHAT IF...

We Are Intergalactic Intelligence?

Copyright © 2021 Hydee Tehana

Hydee Tehana's books may be
ordered through booksellers or Amazon.com.

What If...We Are Intergalactic Intelligence? is book three in the series of What If books.

Trinity Rose Productions, LLC
PO Box 1041
Kealakekua, HI 96750 USA

HydeeTehana.com

ISBN: 978-1-7355836-4-8 (pbk)
ISBN: 978-1-7355836-6-2 (eBook)
ISBN: 978-1-7355836-8-6 (hbk)

Front cover art by Jean-Luc Bozzoli
http://eyewithin.com

Back cover image by Lisa Denning
http://lisadenning.com/

Dedication

This book is dedicated to all those Galactic beings out there in the cosmos and here on planet Earth that are helping to evolve the human race into this next paradigm. It may be a little messy and a bit chaotic, but we got this!

This book is also dedicated to an amazing woman *(and a very advanced and evolved extraterrestrial)*, Joan Ocean, who has brought so much to planet Earth by following her heart, living her joy, and speaking her truth. It is truly an honor to feel the *Master and Goddess* you are. I see you!

"The nature of reality is simple. Everything that exists is made of space, and space is alive and aware. I think this is why people are afraid to be alone. It's because something in them knows they are not alone...ever! They sense there is something there, something enormous, but they can't see or hear it, which scares them. What they're sensing is the vast awareness of space that they are made of and that surrounds, enfolds, and connects them to every living thing that exists...and it's all alive!"

~Penny Kelly

Introduction

This book was inspired by Source and it came on so strong after publishing the first two *What If* books. As I wrote this book, I realized that I wrote this book for me to dive deeper into consciousness and our expansive world as a way to synthesize what I know and understand. There was also a feeling of getting this information out there now to help others as people are ready to dive deeper into what is really out there beyond this Earth and its many mysteries. We are all evolving together.

As I edited this book, I kept seeing one of my multidimensional selves aboard an Arcturian spaceship dictating this book to my human self. It was very clear. This book is an introduction for many of you who have never connected to the Galactic star beings and have no idea about them. This book is also for those who know something about our extraterrestrials, but would like to dive in deeper. Some of you may know more and I invite you to play with your own experiences as you read this book for it is multidimensional in nature, having many truths depending on your perspective.

Also, this book is merely an introduction to some of the advanced extraterrestrial races in the galaxy and is by no means all-inclusive as everything is always evolving and expanding, not to mention that there are infinite galaxies in the Universe. I do refer to advanced races, advanced ET races, advanced civilizations, and Galactics as one in the same, yet not all of these may be evolved spiritually.

The Galactic community is waiting for us to acknowledge them and looking for those who want to be contacted. We are at a point in our history where the old paradigm is falling down and the new paradigm is coming online. Our beliefs are coming into question and our current reality system is opening and shifting. The more we can clear ourselves of our old personal baggage, the more we can go "cosmic" because we open more.

Why reconnect with these Galactic beings of light? We are evolving our consciousness and the collapse of society as we know it is inevitable for it does not hold enough light or the multidimensional possibilities. Our current system holds us in limitation and our collective is done with that. More light will create chaos for a period of time because it is bringing a state of reorganization and healing to Earth.

Perhaps we have hidden our past from ourselves so that we don't scare ourselves!?

Many of us feel that something is missing from life and that is our connection to universal consciousness or oneness. There is a force that connects us all and we are part of it. Some of us may feel like a "fish out of water" being here on Earth, longing to go back to their planet. Yet, many of us came here on a mission with our team to help evolve the human consciousness. Some of us have just forgotten.

The universe is far stranger than most of us can even imagine. I have known that I was from another place my whole life, yet I got sucked into this matrix system of Earth as most of us do. It wasn't until I had my kids that my world began to fall apart in regards to my beliefs and my remembering of the ETs came back. This was a huge relief for me as life suddenly made sense.

That being said, I could now understand different experiences in my life. There was a deep knowing that I came here with my team from the Pleiades to assist in evolving consciousness. I began having more contact from different races of advanced ETs and remembering more of my role in coming to Earth. Often, I felt that I didn't totally belong to any one star system, but to all of them. It was the feeling of being eclectic. There was a peacefulness in knowing and connecting with them...a feeling of "Home."

We humans are made of Intergalactic Intelligence being seeded by at least five other advanced extraterrestrial civilizations. These civilizations are the Pleiadians, Arcturians, Andromedeans, Alpha Centaurians or Venusians, and Sirians. They came together lending their DNA to get what we humans have today. They are all here helping us again (as "parents" often do) now to make a huge leap in consciousness and remember!

I do not claim to be any type of expert in the field of extraterrestrials, but will share what I do know from my experiences, inner knowing, and intuition. Most of the time, I know or feel which group of extraterrestrials are contacting me, yet sometimes I also see or hear them. The cosmos is vast and infinite, yet I still explore and learn as much as I can by expanding my consciousness any chance I get as I find a deeper level of understanding each time.

My intention is not to get you to believe what I believe, but for you to KNOW what is true for you because knowing connects you to the Source or "I AM."

We humans will eventually begin to not identify with a particular country or nation as we realize that we are Earthly beings. Eventually, we will shift our perspective to belonging to this solar system and then perhaps to an even broader Galactic perspective of being from the Milky Way Galaxy. One step at a time, but can you imagine this? We live in exciting times! You chose to come here now just for this expansion and experience.

We have choices in front of us and are being asked what is it that we want to create right now. We have to earn our evolution. We have to earn our technology. We have to earn our consciousness. And we have to earn our invitation to take part in the Galactic community! It will not just be handed to us on a silver platter. Do you want to make this leap in consciousness?

Are you ready?

This is really the time for us to own our power within and to stop having others rule over us because we know the truth. We know who we are and where we came from. We can see through the lies of the material world and we have awakened from our deep slumber.

Our paradigm is shifting.

This book has three parts to it. In part one and two, we look at the ET world and dive into the advanced ET races. Part three covers other topics that I felt guided to add into this book including the topics of time, multidimensionality, plasma physics, wormholes, spaceship technology, our heart, and more. These topics are the foundation of what I would love to have in a school to teach the mysteries of the universe to the world! I would call it a "School of Consciousness."

I like things to be simple and being that I am simple-minded, this book dives into these topics from a straightforward and simple way. You may find yourself reading it again at a different time, finding that you understand it from another perspective.

This is the multidimensional aspect of the book as there are no absolute truths because you will be able to comprehend things from a grander place as your consciousness expands. Truth is all about perspective and the only absolute truth is the "I AM."

As always, please take what resonates and discard the rest. Enjoy an expansive view of our cosmos for we are not alone and we have lots of help!

PART ONE:

THE EXTRATERRESTRIAL WORLD

What If

Are we alone on this planet we call Earth?
What if we aren't alone?

How did we get here?
Did God, Brahma, All That Is, I AM create us?

What about the millions of other planets and galaxies out there?

Are humans just egocentric?
Do we think it is all about us?
Are we just here to live one life and die?
What is life all about?

There are many stories of creation and how we humans came to this planet Earth. Every race on Earth has their own interpretation and creation story. Many of these overlap or are quite similar and show the level of their evolution of consciousness. Our indigenous people often have stories of beings coming from the stars and visiting them who told them many things to help evolve them. Our major religions teach many similar stories with just different names, once you begin to really analyze them. I find it all quite fascinating.

Have you ever stopped to wonder how many galaxies there truly are out there? There are millions of galaxies just in our Milky Way Galaxy alone! This just continues to expand and expand the more we explore what is out there. This universe expands and expands infinitely as Source continues to experience itself in many different ways.

We have been led to believe by many of our religions that this is all there is and when we die, we go to either Heaven or hell. We are taught to believe in God and to obey God if we want eternal life. Believing is different than knowing as knowing is connected to your truth rather than someone's belief. Humans are taught that power is outside ourselves rather than inside ourselves. Religions have really been used against humanity as a way to control us by keeping us in fear.

Advanced extraterrestrial beings know that their power lies within and that if someone believes that power is outside themselves, there will be no evolution of consciousness or spiritual maturity. They know that the cosmos is an eternal field of awareness whose power both creates and destroys. These Galactic beings are looking to "know" God and not to "obey" God as we humans are taught. They also know how powerful our imaginations are and that this is what creates reality where we humans are taught that only what we see with our eyes is real.

Space has unlimited frequencies from which anything can be created anytime you need it. This is the true definition of abundance and what plasma physics is based upon. Advanced extraterrestrials know this (which we will discuss later) and know how to work with frequencies, creating whatever they need. We humans still think there is limited resources, yet this is only true from our limited perspective. As we expand our consciousness, we find this falls away.

What is an advanced race? Is an advanced race flying around in white robes playing harps and singing cumbyeya? What does this really mean? Many people think that there is no more conflict in advanced races when really the conflict is greatly reduced in each individual and as a whole, but that does not mean that they won't defend themselves. Becoming an advanced race or being means that you are able to take in much more information and to process this accurately without defensiveness, have more creative energy, and you also begin to turn into light which allows you to become an eternal being and to move beyond time.

You become ageless.

If you are a humanoid being in this galaxy, you need to be paying attention to the energy around you because it is full of many beings and some of them are not as nice as others. They are all very aware and that is part of the process of becoming an advanced race. They have advanced technology, advanced sciences, advanced relationships, advanced governing systems, and advanced health systems to stay healthy and live forever, so they become very wise indeed.

Advanced Galactic races also know that the goal of life is the development of consciousness to access universal stores of power thus creating experiences that are good for the many. They become eternal beings and work to help other civilizations evolve. Advanced civilizations will never harm any life as they know that all life is precious and sacred. They even know that the malevolent beings are trying to evolve their consciousness.

17

Advanced extraterrestrials love everything as Source.

They are also telepathic and this is standard communication, yet they may have a word or symbol that may stand for a concept (like letters or symbols in some of the hieroglyphics). This concept may contain an entire story, action, or information.

We Earth humans are very spontaneous and advanced races love and hate this at the same time. Diversity is important because it makes a civilization stronger and spontaneity shows other ways of creating that may not have been thought of, if everyone thought the same.

Evolving is different than advancing. To evolve means to advance and reshape your plasma system. When frequency goes up, your pattern changes and evolves. You can be born or brought into an advanced culture and you will get the information just from osmosis of being in that culture. An advanced race may not be evolved in their ethics or how they view life.

Just saying too…the potential that is built into the human to advance is tremendous and we are not inferior to any advanced race. We need to advance ourselves and get out of the lifestyle of hurting and killing each other. We are not less than, but just different than other races. Humans are far from being an advanced race and we are working on this by opening our clairvoyance, clairaudience, clairsentience, etc…for starters. We also need to stop destroying our planet, as we need her!

Remember, the advanced races that we are talking about here are just like us. There are uncountable numbers of human races in the cosmos...yellow, black, white, blue, red, etc...just like on Earth. Humans are self-organizing beings and it is time for us to remember and evolve our consciousness. It is time to open our minds and release our old programs. Life is meant to be full of joy and when we stay connected to our hearts, we are that pure joy that we came in as.

Have ETs visited Earth?
Are they here now?
If so, why are they here?
Why would they want to connect with us?

Do they want to help people of Earth?
Are some ambivalent towards Earthlings?

Have you ever seen a UFO?
Are they real?
Where do they come from?

Is this information being hidden from us?
If so, why is that?
Is it our own governments hiding this?
Why is there secrecy around all of this?

There are many records of extraterrestrials visiting our Earth in petroglyph records and other histories throughout our civilizations. They walk among us and some of us know that we have connections to other galaxies. We are currently being invited to remember our connections to the larger Galactic community and to remember our origins.

We are in a special time right now of shifting paradigms into a more expanded consciousness. There are many advanced civilizations here helping us right now whether we know it or not. The Galactics are our family and many of us are beginning to remember.

I find it interesting that some governments here on Earth are open with their citizens about extraterrestrials. Years ago in a seminar, I was talking to a woman from Mexico who told me how she knew ETs and UFOs were real. She said the Mexican government openly acknowledged them. I was shocked as she told me this as our government in the United States has hidden this for years.

Advanced ET races that are here on Earth have tried to announce themselves, but many of our governments have not allowed this. Unfortunately, our governments have not followed through with their end of the bargain, so many extraterrestrials have been contacting us individually as they want to be able to move around freely. It seems there has been a complete cosmic cover up to keep information from us.

Apparently, some of the Alpha Centauri beings who were originally from Venus, lived in Paradise, California and were going to announce themselves to the public. Our government did not like this and caused massive destruction to the city of Paradise by way of fires caused from direct energy weapons and more. I have heard this from a few people, but have not verified it myself.

There was also a man by the name of Urander Olivera from Brazil who was working with the Pleiadians. They asked him to gather seventy people or so as they would pick him up in plain sight in 1998. A Pleiadian ship arrived and he walked into their light beam which took him onto the ship. Seventy witnesses saw this, but nothing was ever said more publicly about this.

This should have been headline news!

There were spaceship crashes in Louisiana and Germany after World War I that our governments and other breakaway groups got a hold of. They began reverse engineering the technology of these ships. This has been recently declassified in CIA online archives. It seems true that both our governments and other breakaway groups have advanced technology of how to fly spaceships, teleport, control the weather, and even time travel.

According to a series of war documents and other declassified documents, Hitler's engineers had state-of-the-art battle tanks, rockets, flying saucers, anti-gravity technology, and some type of aerial vehicles known as "light balls" back in the 1930s! They also investigated advanced propulsion technologies including missile and powerful turbines developed by Viktor Schauberger.

The Nazi's searched remote places on Earth for devices, ancient manuscripts, the Arc of the Covenant, and other paranormal technologies just like in the movie series of *Indiana Jones*. Is truth revealed in our movies? Several authors maintain that Nazi Germany explored Antarctica in 1938 and beyond, where many Nazi leaders supposedly fled after WWII.

There is much that could be said about the spaceship that crashed in Roswell, New Mexico in 1947, but our government continues to not acknowledge this saying it was a weather balloon. Much talk has been around this crash and many believe this was one of our own spaceships that our military had crashed.

Linda Moulton Howe has been investigating UFOs, abductions, and crop circles for many years. She was able to obtain some of the metal from the Roswell crash and took it to many scientists to see what the metal was made of. None of them knew what it was and said that some of the metals used should not have been able to be bonded together.

What do the ETs know about bonding metals?
What happens when you bond Magnesium, Zinc, and Bismuth together?

A number of secret space programs exist within the governments of Russia, Germany, USA, and China. Do you remember the warning from President Eisenhower who said, "Beware of the Military Industrial Complex?" Part of our military broke off and became the "MIC" which explored many advanced technologies. Some people refer to this as part of the "cabal" or "illuminati."

President Trump in 2019 announced the creation of "Space Force" as a new branch of the military in an attempt to catch up with space, but this will probably not go that far because the intention is to have armed forces in space. Advanced civilizations are not interested in this because they don't won't more war added to space as they are trying to stop war in space already.

I have seen spaceships with my own eyes and it truly is an incredible sighting. One time, I was with my daughter and her sixth grade class on a camping trip in Hawaii. It was at dusk and suddenly I heard the sixth graders yelling, "ETs! Come pick me up! Aliens! Get me outta here!" I came running out and looked up in the sky seeing seven lightships hovering in the sky.

I knew immediately that they were spaceships and ran to grab my camera. It felt like they were from the Pleiades. They stayed for a few more seconds before disappearing. I did get a couple poor shots of them. The funny thing to me was another mom witnessed the whole thing. She turned to me once they left and said, "Those were planes, right?"

I said, "Nope. Those were spaceships."

She answered saying, "No, those were planes and they all just turned, so we can't see their lights." Another father who was an airplane pilot was standing there with us and said to her, "Those were not planes. Those were spaceships!"

What would happen if ETs are real?
Would it mess with our beliefs and religions?

Is it hidden to keep us from expanding our consciousness?

What if they are real and want to help us?
Think of the possibilities!

What if extraterrestrials are real in our reality? What would that do to how we think and operate in the world today? This would expand our thinking and our consciousness to realize that there is much more out there than we humans on a ball in the middle of the cosmos all by ourselves! The foundation of our beliefs would collapse and we would begin to question what is real.

We would begin to see life differently as we would connect with our brothers and sisters of the cosmos and learn from them. It would connect us to our origins of the truth to how we came to be on the planet Earth. We would not feel alone.

There is a huge paradigm shift happening right now on our planet and all our beliefs that we have held into place are being questioned. A paradigm is merely beliefs, thoughts, and information that create a reality system. What is true for us? Who has decided what it is that we are to believe? Where did religion itself come from?

Our religions are man-made belief systems that attempt to tell us how humans came to be, how we are to act, and what we are to believe. There is typically a threat through fear to get us to buy into religion if we don't believe. These are merely systems used to control the larger population, so that they don't question their true origins of where they came from.

These take away our power and get us to believe in something that is outside ourselves. Many people are waking up and taking their power back by connecting to their truth within. The Galactic community is cheering us on and ready to connect with us if we ask. They have already contacted many humans and are helping us to expand our consciousness as we remember our connections to the larger part of the whole.

We are in a time where it is important to connect with our Galactic brothers and sisters so we can make the leap in consciousness as humanity is facing many issues with our sun and our planet. There are those extraterrestrials who are benevolent and wanting to help us as well as those extraterrestrials who are malevolent and want to control us. It is important for us to discern the energies of these beings and trust what we know is right for us.

What an amazing time that we chose to be alive and experience!

What if there are ETs that go around seeding planets?
If so, why are they doing this?
What are they trying to create?
Who seeded this planet?

How long does it take to get life on a planet?
How do they do this?

Is this why ancient cultures talk about the "gods" from the skies?

Is it ETs coming from other systems to check on us?
Are we their children?
Where did they come from?

We are the dust of Earth that has been blended with the cosmic stuff of the Star Gods. Many of us are starseeds and are connected to other star systems. It appears that humans today are from a genetic engineering program with starseed DNA from advanced extraterrestrial civilizations that have advanced technology.

As I mentioned before, humanity is Intergalactic Intelligence made up of at least five different extraterrestrial civilizations. Those include the Pleiadians, Arcturians, Andromedeans, Alpha Centaurians/Venusians, and the Sirians. All of these Galactic civilizations have lent their DNA to make us today. This is the fifth time of planet Earth that humans have been seeded here and this current system has been going on for 60-80,000 years which is all documented on petroglyphs around the world.

In this current seeding, there has been some mutations in humans over the last 12,000 to 25,000 years because of the sun's changes and conditions affecting us and our dynamic planet Earth.

There is evidence that has been found on our planet of skeletons of giants, tiny humanoids, elongated skulls, man-beasts with horns and tails, and mermaids/mermen. This was being discovered in the early 1900s and beyond with some of these discoveries being printed in newspapers and magazines. Eventually, those in power decided to hide these from the public, allowing only what they permitted to be published. Much has been hidden in the Smithsonian and those associated with them because it would challenge our religions and belief systems. We would discover our extraterrestrial ancestry.

What if the gods of our religions are really just advanced humans from other extraterrestrial planets? There are many depictions of spaceships or beings in spaceships in medieval art. At a certain point, the Catholic church forbid people to look at the skies. Was there spaceships flying around and connecting with the humans on Earth?

Absolutely.

Those civilizations that seeded us come back often and check on us to see how we are progressing and assist us. Right now, there are many of them here helping us to evolve our consciousness and remember our origins to the stars. As a Galactic civilization grows spiritually and technologically, they begin exploring the universe and seeding other planets with life. It isn't easy to get life going and life is truly precious.

This is truly the "I AM" wanting to know itself more and more with experiences in an ever-expanding infinite universe.

Are ETs here to teach us?
To remind us?
To help us?

Can they help us?

How do they live?
Are there good ones and bad ones?
Are some advanced and others not?

Do some align with life?
Do some try to advance life?
Do some align with death?

How do we not see them?
Perhaps we do, but we just forgot?

The last greatest war going on right now on Earth is a war on our consciousness. It is happening right now between those that wish to control us and those that wish to help us evolve and free us. We are close to stepping into our power and expanding our consciousness. There are those light beings who want to see us make the leap in consciousness and those dark beings who want to keep our consciousness stalled so that they can continue to control us. There is a great clash right now between good vs. evil or between the light and dark forces for our consciousness.

Right now on Earth, we are at a point of evolve or die. If we don't see the bigger picture and make the leap in consciousness, our civilization as we know it will be destroyed because many of us are aligned with death. Humans think that all we do is eat, sleep, work, be entertained, and eventually die. We need to decide how our consciousness is aligned and we will be led down that path. This is what it really means to awaken…we stop being sheep and begin to think for ourselves!

Advanced ETs are not here to "save" us as we need to wake up and take the initiative to "save" ourselves. They will help us if we ask, but will not do it for us. We need to begin examining the system we are living in with its beliefs and constructs. We look fear in the face and decide that we will stand in our power instead of being in fear. We came here for this time…this leap in consciousness to learn Christ or Buddha consciousness (connecting to the "God" within) and create our new Earth with new belief systems, new sciences, and new technologies.

We are those ETs from other advanced civilizations who chose to come here in human form this time to help this evolution of consciousness. Many of us have forgotten our true mission here on Earth, yet many of us are starting to remember. ETs have very advanced ways of living in the cosmos as they have expanded their consciousness and are in their power.

Advanced ETs know that the cosmos is an eternal field of awareness and it has the power to both create and destroy. Advanced extraterrestrials want to know "God" on a deeper and deeper level as it just keeps going and going. According to Penny Kelly (who remembers her life in the Pleiades) in her Patreon videos, they know that the "goal" of life is develop your consciousness in order to access universal power and to use this to create experiences that are good for the many. This is also echoed in the book series, *Life and Teaching of the Masters of the Far East* by Baird Spalding. This is quite opposite for most of us humans whose goal is to usually just be happy and free.

Humans tend to believe because of our religions that "God" created our universe and everything with it. We often believe that there is a heaven or hell depending if we believe in Jesus or not, or if we are good. Here is the kicker…Jesus was a title and was given to many people years ago as they advanced and evolved their consciousness according to the books, *The Christ Conspiracy* by Acharya S, *When God was a Woman* by Merlin Stone, and the series, *History: Fiction or Science?* by Anatoly Fomenko. The word "Jesus" means your inner teacher and healer.

In fact, there used to be many "Jesus" people around with extraordinary powers and the church decided to create a religion to control the people with one figure named Jesus. They knew there were too many people coming into their power and evolving their consciousness, so they made up religions, killing millions who didn't follow them. This truly was the dark ages putting a huge damper on our consciousness.

—

Advanced ETs know that their power is inside themselves and this is how you evolve your power and become spiritually mature. Advanced extraterrestrials are fully aware of what is going on around them for if they don't, they may suffer an accident. Humans tend to look outside themselves for someone to tell them what to do or how to think and tend to think that things happen to us like we are victims.

When you are an advanced extraterrestrial, you know that the source of all energy is frequencies and fields. You know that space has unlimited frequencies which can create anything. There is no lack or limits like most of us humans believe. Think about that for a moment…there is no lack or limits, meaning there are no limited resources as we are taught to believe on Earth.

Advanced extraterrestrials know that reality is subjective and only becomes objective when two or more agree on a perception. They know that they are responsible for what they are creating and participating in as reality is entirely malleable. Their thoughts are creating everything. There is no victim mentality. Abraham-Hicks speaks of this all the time in her books and seminars.

This is very opposite to what most humans believe which is that what you see is reality and imagination is make-believe. Most believe that dreams or daydreams don't matter and this is reinforced when we are children.

Imagination is everything as you are putting your energy into creating a new reality as you feel into it. Science is showing this through plasma physics as it shows how this immediately begins to pull energy together which will eventually become solid form with enough attention to it based on electric, magnetic, and gravitational energies.

What do you daydream about?
What are you creating?

Have you ever seen a "light" being? Perhaps you have seen your "guardian angel?" Ever talk to your "spirit guide?" Those are parts of yourself that are helping you as we are multidimensional. You exist on many levels. You may have shut down your ability to see the other realms because others didn't see them.

Ever seen a spaceship or cloud ship? You may knowingly see and talk to advanced ET races already and know that you are not from here. You may already know your mission and visit the ships regularly for updates and upgrades. There are very advanced light beings out there ready to help you if you ask for help, but you need to take the initiative.

Start with just asking for an acceleration of your consciousness.

What type of worlds are out there?
Does the cosmos expand forever?
Is it unlimited?

There are many types of fascinating worlds out in the cosmos that go on and on forever. The Pleiadians and others keep exploring the universe and they say it is never-ending as we keep creating it. It is just like when we wonder and ask, "What other creatures are in the deep blue sea?" More creatures are created and found because we are creating this!

According to Penny Kelly, who has explored a lot of the cosmos, she says that you can categorize all the worlds into a few types of worlds. These are barren worlds, weird worlds, despair worlds, and beautiful worlds. On these barren worlds, there is literally nothing. Very old and powerful beings live on these barren worlds who don't want much to maintain. There are beautiful worlds like our Earth world all over the cosmos and these are for younger beings who want to maintain this type of reality system.

Then, you have the weird worlds where there are strange creatures on them. Some of them are like a Disney type worlds and others are like the movie, *The Matrix*, where you are literally being chased as soon as you enter it. You stand on a dolphin picture on the ground to go in and out of this type of world.

There are also the despair worlds where everything is dark and horrible. It is like a hell world where thoughts are very dense and negative. These are opposite of the Heaven worlds which would be part of the beautiful worlds.

Advanced extraterrestrials who are spiritually evolved as well as technologically evolved are busy evolving their consciousness by helping the cosmos evolve in many worlds. Their consciousness is ever expanding as they find new perspectives on how to view Source.

Advanced ETs do not use money nor do they need money on their worlds. They know how to create what it is that they need by understanding plasma physics which we will discuss later in this book. They may incarnate in another world to help it evolve as many of us are these ETs who came to help evolve Earth. We are working in every facet of society.

The cosmos are forever expansive as the "I Am" or Source is forever playing and having fun learning more and more about itself.

What is "the light?"
Who is "the light?"
Where did it come from?

How did this all start?
Who decided to move "the soup" into form?

Why aren't we all just still part of "the soup" or "the oneness?"

Who first made the sound?
Did sound precede light?

Sound was what first started the universe and then there was light. Everything was and is total space. Space is what I call "the oneness" or "the soup," as Penny Kelly or Mehran Keshe calls it. It is total bliss, love, and one with Source. Space is better defined as the location aspect of mind and mind is the awareness property of space. The question of space/mind is really how did it ever begin to move or go from nothingness to everything to making form like us? What began it all?

I have asked Source and there is a deep knowing yet I cannot put it into words. There is a sense that Source wanted to experience itself over and over again. Still, I wonder why I ever left the oneness as I have memories of being there and being asked by Source to come here. Perhaps the bigger part of me is still there and truly is, as everything is connected.

There are times where I have experienced the bliss of "the oneness" and in those moments, I know everything…everything makes sense. I am able to keep this knowing for quite some time, but it fades in this veiled world until it happens to me again!

As we leave Source which is mind/space, we move into consciousness and energy where consciousness is the feeling aspect of energy and energy is the movement of consciousness. From here, we go from waves of frequencies into intelligent particles where those particles begin to group together. They begin to form patterns and these patterns begin to make up forms like animals, humans, plants, planets, galaxies, etc…

Source is "the light" and is powerful, loving, and total bliss. When you are in its presence, this light envelopes you and this is what you truly are. It is what many call God, Source, Spirit, All That Is, I AM, etc…

We are also made of light as we come from Source and we can develop our light by expanding our consciousness. We can bring in more light by bringing in more electricity as we are electromagnetic beings through exercise, good food and water, Earthing, and sunlight. If you can see the lights around people (auras) or things, you will see that some have huge auras and others have very little which shows you how healthy someone is.

When we die, we can go to many places and many talk about seeing "the light" as it pulls them closer. You will be drawn to go into "the light" as it is total bliss and you just can't help but feel so much love from the light. Penny Kelly says that you should have a conversation with "the light" before you go into it or you will go into another life either on Earth or some other reality system. This is why some people say, "it is all a dream." You literally "wake up" in another reality system. Eckhart Tolle talks about this as well.

What should you say to "the light?" Ask questions of "the light" like, "Am I done here, where am I going, what am I doing, what am I learning, what if I go here, etc…" You will receive answers and decide where you want to go next. Stay very present and aware. It is really up to you and what you want to experience. Everything is conscious and listening.

What if this is all just a game?!

What would you like to experience? Do you want to go forwards or backwards in "time" on Earth and experience a life in the Roman days or Goddess days or a future time? Do you want to experience something different altogether and go to another planet or reality system? Time is just a grouping of specific frequencies in one location, so match that frequency and you can go there!

All of our stories and myths really say the same thing of taking us back into magnificent love. We are made of this amazing, intelligent light and it is the becoming of light consciously and on purpose that makes us a "divine being." Stay connected to the light as it can move us past death and into the category of being an immortal.

Death is truly a mistake in thinking.

PART TWO:

EXTRATERRESTRIAL RACES

What If

Where is the Pleiades?
Can we see it with our naked eye?
Who are the Pleiadians?
Did they seed this planet?

What is it like there?
What do they look like?

The Pleiades is in the Taurus constellation and is 444 light years away from Earth. You can find the Pleiades in the sky as a cluster of stars that are up from the Orion's belt. The Pleiadians are a very advanced race with a very evolved consciousness and many of them are here on Earth in human bodies helping humans remember their Galactic connections and to evolve our consciousness.

Are you one of them?

Our sun orbits the Pleiades once every 25,860 years and reaches the midpoint of the photon belt (which is a huge toroidal belt of interdimensional light) every 12,500 years. This is where we are right now and massive amounts of light are streaming onto our Earth. Pleiadians have seeded life on many planets like our Earth and have connections to many civilizations on Earth like the Polynesians, Mayans, American Indians, Japan, Egypt, Lemuria, and Atlantis. In fact, Subaru is Japanese for the Pleiades!

The temple of Hathor at Dendera in Egypt was dedicated to the Pleiades and has the Pleiades on the ceiling. Greece was also very connected to the Pleiades. Alcyone is the central star/sun of the Pleiades constellation. Our solar system moves around Alcyone of the Pleiades photon belt which takes 26,000 years as shown on the Mayan calendar.

Pleiadians live for thousands of years and know how to reset and heal their frequencies as needed. Their system is over two billion years old according to Penny Kelly who knows that she has another life going on there. Remember, we are multidimensional and can live lives in many places concurrently, which we will get into later in this book.

Randy Masters, who is a sound healer, also knows that he is from this system and remembers his life there as it is currently another parallel life for him. He talks about the sacred geometry and crystals used for their homes.

I am very connected to the Pleiades and have been my whole life. This is one of the last parts of this book that I wrote and I find it interesting because I deeply know about the Pleiadians, but have trouble finding the words to describe my experiences with them. It is like they are a part of me, yet there are many of the advanced races that I absolutely love and feel the same.

Anyways, like most of us, I forgot my connection to them during my teenage years, but still stared at their constellation when I would look up at the stars in the evenings. There was something so familiar and I wanted to know them again, but I was "knee deep" in this reality system.

It wasn't until I had my daughter in my thirties when I remembered I had connections to the stars. One day when she was five, my daughter was having a session with a woman who was a medium. In the session, she mentioned that there were these "tall light beings" in the session who were healing my daughter who called themselves "The Pleiadians."

This was all I needed to hear and I knew in that instant, my connection to them. It was like a remembering and alignment took place for me. I am not alone here and I knew that I belonged to a team of Pleiadians who came here to help evolve consciousness. I continued to remember more and saw that I also have a parallel life there in the Pleiades.

P'Taah is a Pleiadian man who has contacted me from time to time as one of my guides. He answers my questions, shares his wisdom, and has a great sense of humor. I have found that he is also in contact with other Pleiadian starseeds on the planet right now.

There are so many books that have been written about the Pleiadeans and many that have been channeled as well. Books by Barbara Marciniak or Christine Day who were both contacted by the Pleiadians to remind us of our connections to them and what we are doing here.

In the book, *The Promise* by Dr. Fred Bell, the Pleiadians told Fred that they are from time eternal. In the book, he met a Pleiadian woman named Semjase who was very powerful and had long golden brown hair, large emerald green eyes, white skin, and wore a silver one-piece suit. When she spoke or telepathed, it was musical in nature. She assisted him on his mission here on Earth.

Also in this book, Semjase wanted to make it clear that Pleiadians are not "higher beings, gods, or angels." They have just evolved their consciousness and are related to us humans. Just as a reminder, all advanced races have those who are benevolent and malevolent just like we humans do. The majority of the Pleiadians are benevolent.

Let's look at the Pleiadian civilization. The Pleiadians as well as many other advanced civilizations organize themselves with a series of councils. They have family councils, local councils, regional councils, all the way up to Galactic councils. This is a way of making sure that everyone has a way to get help, receive understanding, get information, or to resolve a problem. The councils also watch to see which children are showing different types of skill sets, so that they can help nurture the child to move in that direction of what interests them. This is important for their future leaders, spaceship commanders, scientists, musicians, etc... Some of them will be the cosmonauts on spaceships exploring the vast cosmos as they are mapping our infinite cosmos.

The Pleiadians look very human and are about ten to twelve feet tall. I have seen many with light skin, blond hair, and blue eyes. They can actually change forms if they want to...like shapeshifting. Sometimes, they have hair and sometimes they don't.

Pleiadians will only do what they love to do and they want absolute freedom with creativity. There is no privacy as all are telepathic.

In regards to sex and relationships, humans still have sex and babies where among the advanced races, babies are mostly clones or hybrids according to Penny Kelly. Some of them put babies into human races and allow them to reproduce. Some of them use test tubes. Once the baby is born, advanced races begin to teach and train that new consciousness to help the new one expand. Humans are valued for their reproduction as many of the advanced races don't have the capacity to have children.

Among advanced races, relationships and sexuality are totally different. Pleiadians want sexual compatibility. It is not like us humans where sex sells everything and love relationships are a cornerstone for us. Kundalini is sometimes awakened by a sexual experience and if it goes all the way up through all our chakras, we will have an expanded and awakened consciousness. This allows for alignment with the "I AM" or Source for you to bring this energy into your work.

Sex is all energetic for the advanced races where they blend with another energy system to the point that you cannot tell if that is your energy system or theirs. Breathwork is part of this. Love relationships are part of synchronizing consciousness more than anything. A simple touch is used to create an orgasm in the advanced races which can align your whole system and reset your frequencies. It is used for healing rather than sexual experiences. It is like an electrocution.

In advanced races, children's lives, intelligence, and education are supremely important. They know how to help the child advance and teachers are the highest honor for the Pleiadians. You cannot give birth and raise children on your own. It is a community process which the whole community values dearly for they know it is the lifeblood of their civilization.

As children grow in the Pleiadian culture, a Pleiadian child may be one hundred and twenty years old and go to live with another advanced race for ten years to learn more from them. It is like a study abroad system here on Earth. Then, they will come back and share what they learned with the whole community.

They are very into frequencies and music. Pleiadians wear clothing (skin suits) that is engineered to harmonize according to Penny Kelly. It is like a frequency generator that puts off music and color. This will generate a reaction and feeling to make other people happy. Pleiadians always think of others and how they are affecting others. They have light and sound shows for just entertainment.

How about we bring this to Earth?

Penny Kelly also said that the average age of a Pleiadian is seven to eight hundred years old. Some of their "national treasures" are ancient beings who are walking libraries. They store their consciousness and have the technology for this. They can regenerate the body as they need to, becoming eternal beings.

Think about this.
You don't lose all your wisdom by dying.
You become an immortal being.

Pleiadians want to help others in the galaxy however they can, as many advanced civilizations do. They are playful and humorous. Pleiadians love music, dancing, and movement. The dancing is a fluid environment kind of like fish in the ocean or synchronized swimming while being aware of everyone. It increases their consciousness. They are also incredibly creative, gentle, and powerful. Pleiadians like to play out dramas together rather than watch movies according to Penny Kelly.

What if instead of money, we had beauty as our criteria for our world other than what we have here? We need permission to have beauty and need cooperation to make this work. We need to let go of competition and give ourselves permission to do this.

Are you ready? The Pleiadians are very present on our planet and in our consciousness. Ask for them from your heart space and they will assist you. We have so much help!

Who are the Arcturians?
Did they seed this planet?

Where is Arcturus?
Can we see it from Earth?

What are they doing here?
Are they helping us?

The Arcturians are from the Bootes constellation which is 36.7 light years away and you can see it with your naked eye. If you follow the handle of the big dipper down, you will land on a bright star called Arcturus. It is the fourth brightest star that we can see in our night's sky and eighteen times greater than our sun. It is said to be over ten billion years old and a red supergiant star.

One of the many advanced civilizations who seeded the Earth this time around, the Arcturians are on a mission to help us succeed by increasing planetary consciousness. They work for the light following universal laws while protecting life, intelligence, and freedom all over the Milky Way Galaxy. Arcturians will destroy any malevolent beings who encroaches on freedom. The Arcturians are currently quite present in our atmosphere protecting us from malevolent beings or "feeders" as they are sometimes known. The "feeders" feed off of negative emotions like fear and chaos.

The Arcturians are a very advanced intergalactic civilization both technologically and spiritually. There are many of us from Arcturus living here on the Earth right now helping to expand our consciousness and make the leap into a new paradigm. Some of them are working in our governments and with our financial system knowing they are from Arcturus, but are Earth humans.

Some of this may sound a bit like *Star Trek,* but perhaps this is where the show came from? According to Tom Kenyon in *The Arcturian Anthology*, Sanat Kumara is the starship commander of the Arcturian ship, *Athena*, which currently resides in our galaxy and has lots of armaments with complex technology for battle. There are many other ships here as well. Sanat Kumara is multidimensional (as are we!) and has been a long time protector of many galaxies. He landed another spaceship on Mt. Kamara in Koyoto, Japan over ten million years ago. There is a model of his ship there reminding others of his time here. He also brought Reiki to Earth.

The Arcturians are reminding us to get into our hearts and out of our heads. They know that as we move upward in our vibratory states of consciousness, we perceive the physical world quite differently. Many advanced races are helping us reconnect with nature or it will destroy us as our world is in transition and we have forgotten that we are part of nature, not rulers of nature.

We are in the middle of a battle in both the etheric and physical worlds between those that want to free us and those that want to imprison us. Many of us came here just for this particular time because we are helping to free Earth and make the leap in consciousness. There are many solar winds or flares that are bringing these winds of change which activate humans and shift our frequencies.

The Arcturians (like many of the advanced Galactic races) can shapeshift their energies and can look different in how we perceive them. This is also due to how the plasma forms our energy signatures in different dimensions. Sometimes, I have seen them as small humanoid beings with big eyes and pointy ears while other times, I have seen them about five feet or so. Tom Kenyon has seen them as humanoids with square heads or horse like faces.

We humans are Intergalactic Intelligence. Humans have many extraordinary gifts that are waiting to unfold and flower. Some of us already know this as you may have had a kundalini experience or still have your memories intact. The Arcturians will help if you ask and will activate your light body in the Arcturian Corridor.

The Arcturian Corridor is a tunnel of light that serves as an interdimensional portal or stargate that connects to our multidimensional self. It is a "waystation" and we travel through the corridor to Earth and to other star systems. As a "waystation," it is used as a way for our nonphysical consciousness to get used to physicality. Dr. Suzanne Lie goes into more detail about this in *Journey Through the Arcturian Corridor*.

The Arcturians offer us healing whenever we need it by asking to go to a higher dimension with them and work with their high dimensional healers. This can help us to expand our consciousness. The Arcturians have been exploring intergalactically for over one hundred million years according to Tom Kenyon. They also have twenty-four strands of DNA and use re-genesis chambers to live incredibly long lives. Dr. Norma Milanovich, who wrote *We, The Arcturians*, discusses some of this in her book as well as the starship, *Athena*.

When the Arcturians showed up in my life, I was headed out on a humpback whale trip in the Dominican Republic with my son. I kept staring at this one star which turned out to be Arcturus. Later during this trip, a friend of mine handed me this book called *How the Arcturians are healing Planet Earth* by Wayne Brewer which was all about how the Arcturians were protecting the Earth.

This book went on to talk about calling in the Arcturians and working with them to remove negative beings from our Earth plane. I was skeptical, but thought I would try it next time I felt there was negative energies. Well, I did this at the end of our trip in the Dominican Republic at the airport and found that I disturbed a "hornet's nest" of dark energy below the airport. It was so strong that it completely shut down the airport and they cancelled everyone's flights for the rest of the day!

Turns out that I didn't call in the Arcturians and follow the procedure outlined in the book quite right. I knew exactly what happened and this showed me how real and powerful dark energies are. This also showed me how real the Arcturians are! I began working with my beloved Arcturians for years now on and off. They have taught me so much and I know I have lived and studied among these amazing, advanced beings who are helping all of us.

If you feel called, ask to connect with them as there are many of us Earth humans doing so now. They have continued to show me that the problems we have are actually here to awaken us. As we let go of our old patterns and baggage, we find that our human bodies are a grounding point on the physical plane connected to our huge, multidimensional form. If you feel called, allow the Arcturians to help show you the light that you are and become one with it.

Your world will never been the same.
You will remember what you truly are.
This is your highest path to pure consciousness.

Where are the Hathors from?
Who are the Hathors?
How did they get here?

What are they like?
Are they kind?
What do they look like?
Were they back in Egyptian times?

The Hathors are some of my favorite beings. I just get this big smile on my face as I feel their love and see their faces. Hathors have beautiful faces with big loving eyes and their ears remind me of the ears that cows have. Their nature is energetic and interdimensional.

I have always had a draw to Egypt my whole life and I feel it was partly the Hathors that were calling me there. When I arrived at the Hathor temple in Dendera, Egypt, it felt so familiar and there was a softness to it. Also, Hator is also an Egyptian goddess of bliss, joy, sacred sexuality, dance, and fertility, but very much connected to the Hathors. This is much of what the Hathors represent along with their great sense of humor. They led many of their initiates to North Africa and Egypt after the destruction of Atlantis and Lemuria.

One thing I noticed when coming to the Hathor temple is how huge the entrance was and I realized it was because these Hathors are fifteen feet tall and would come and go from this temple. They energies are still present today and I found it fascinating that almost every Hathor face had been removed and destroyed on the temple. Our guide said it was because the Hathor energy from their collective was so strong and those with clairvoyance could see these beings were still there with their energy coming through their faces.

Wow.
Powerful!

This reminds me of why many indigenous and other spiritual people don't like to have their pictures taken.

Now, according to Tom Kenyon in his book, *The Hathor Material,* the Hathors told him that they came from another universe through the portal of Sirius into our galaxy stopping at Venus first for some raw materials and gasses before coming back to Earth. The Arcturians held the space for them by protecting them with four of their spaceships. The Hathors travel in nautilus ships and have been to Earth many times to help humans evolve.

The Hathors are intergalactic travelers who are non-interventionalists and avoid confrontation by moving themselves up and down the energy spectrum from fourth dimension to twelfth dimension. They do not engage in battle, but simply disappear from the space just like the Sasquatch. The Hathors ascended as a collective instead of individually like the Arcturians and live in a vibratory state of love and ecstasy.

They are here on Earth now releasing vibrations of love and introducing seeds of harmony and balance while the Arcturians protect them. The Hathors teach about connecting with nature, sound, and vibrational healing as much is still stored in stones. They are able to travel in and out of space and time without really entering it by moving up and down the light spectrum. The Hathors are androgenous beings who are in perfect balance both magnetically and electrically.

The Hathors are reminding us that we only see one percent of the universe as there is still so much out there. Our bodies are made up of the cosmos. Nature holds the secrets and many of us have studied with the Hathors before. The Hathors are not here to save us, but are simply are elder brothers and sisters helping us to evolve our consciousness.

My most recent communication with them was where they were showing me how reality is malleable. They repeated this over and over. I was seeing their nautilus ship, in my mind's eye, going in and out of our reality system working with our frequencies. Our reality system looked like a gelatinous cloud that would close upon itself once they entered or once they left. Again, I kept hearing, "Reality is malleable."

Fascinating.

There was more that they imparted to me and I kept looking at their spaceships. Their ships look like a nautilus and I realized that these are shaped like galaxies. When I looked up more about the nautilus the next day, I found that the nautilus follows the Fibonacci sequence which is found in nature like in the pine cones, cauliflower, and hurricanes. Within the nautilus is the Golden Ratio which is found in all living things.

What do the Hathors know about this shape and their spaceships? One could also think of the nautilus as the ever expansion of consciousness as it gets bigger and bigger.

So much more to learn from them!

Are the Venusians from Venus?
Who are the Venusians?
Did they seed this planet?

What was it like there?
Are they still there?
Are they benevolent?
What do they look like?

Did they leave Venus for Alpha Centauri?
Are they helping us?

Venus is 25 million miles away from Earth and has a surface temperature of 800 degrees Fahrenheit. It also spins the opposite direction of Earth. There are reports of beings living inside of Venus.

The Venusians are from Venus and one of the races who seeded life on planet Earth. They are the original water people. The Venusians had a beautiful, lush planet at one time, but our Sun destroyed Venus with one of its cyclical micronovas. The Venusians knew of the impeding micronova and fled to Earth to avoid destruction.

The Venusians enjoyed the Earth, but knew that they would have to leave Earth eventually when the Sun had another micronova. They moved into the inner Earth and began to cultivate life inside the planet as many beings do on other planets since it is more stable than the surface. As they advanced their consciousness more, they were able to begin exploring other galaxies in search of a new home.

They eventually found a star system called Alpha Centauri which is a system of three stars called A, B, and Proxima Centauri. Alpha Centauri A is a younger star and Meton is one of their seven planets. They took residence with one of these stars as their sun and it has seven planets that all are now inhabited. It is four light years away from Earth according to the Alpha Centaurians. Proxima Centauri is another stable sun further out and is 4.2 light years away from Earth.

The Venusians began transporting their people there as well as some animals and began to cultivate life there. They also left some of their people in inner Earth to help the surface Earth people and to report back to those on Alpha Centauri. Venusians are still here today helping us.

Valiant Thor and his team are some of those helping us on the surface to expand our consciousness. They contacted our United States government in the 1950's under President Eisenhower to show a different way to be in the world without war. Valiant Thor stayed in the Pentagon, meeting with many government officials all over the world, but was turned down as our governments did not want to give up their power.

Dr. Frank Stranges was contacted by Valiant Thor and they worked together attempting to help humans on Earth which he wrote about in his book called *Stranger at the Pentagon*. He witnessed many of Valiant Thor's superpowers and went on his spaceship. Together, they kept trying to help us wake up and Valiant Thor vowed to remain on Earth until we make the great leap in consciousness. He is able to go in and out of the inner Earth and make contact with those of us who are ready to help.

I have always loved Venus and it has been in the past year where they have announced themselves into my life. One day while at the beach, I looked up in the sky and there was a very large planet right above me. It was daytime and very sunny. I was so surprised to be able to visually see this and I just felt into it. When I walked back to my car, I got my phone app out to see what planet it was.

Venus!

After this, everything Venus began coming to me and reminding me. I didn't even know there were Venusians out there!

I had a life on Venus that I saw in a past life which felt like eons ago. I was a water creature being…an amphibious looking human with translucent blue, green, and pink with rainbow in my aura. My feet were webbed and I was traveling around the cosmos learning from other civilizations. The planet was waterous and incredible. How could I have forgotten my connection to Venus?!

How many others of us are from Venus?

The people of Earth are descendants from the people of Venus who were the original water beings. Is this why many of us love the water?

In the book, *Beyond the Light Barrier* by Elizabeth Klarer, Elizabeth describes her relationship with a man from Alpha Centauri named Akon in the 1950s and 1960s. Her story tells of a deep and loving relationship with Akon and her remembrance of living on Meton in Alpha Centauri. She tells of how their spaceships work, what their community is like, other types of advanced technologies, and how life is aboard spaceships. Elizabeth and Akon had an agreement to meet on Earth and for her to birth a son with their genes together to help strengthen their lineage since she was also of Venusian descent.

She explained that the Venusians know that light is all of creation and that we are light along with "God" or Source being light. They commune with all of nature and need no religion or money. They live in total balance and harmony.

Elizabeth had a big job here on Earth and was to help humans evolve their consciousness by showing our connections to the Galactics. Unfortunately, most of our governments wanted to kidnap her because she had a son with Akon (she was fifty years old) who ended up being born on Alpha Centauri in 1958.

This book describes what Earth is expecting in the upcoming years as we approach another micronova. It is time for us to pay attention to this as we surface dwellers will need to get off the Earth.

Elizabeth spoke to many governments throughout the world including the UN. She talked about how the Venusians had overcome the aging process and most importantly, they control their thoughts as they know that this creates everything. They also use their mind to navigate with their conscious spaceships. She died in the 1990s, but you can watch her documentary interview on YouTube.

We have so much help trying to get us to expand our consciousness. Will we accept this help and move past our power hungry ways?

On October 18, 2020, I hiked into a beautiful valley on the Big Island of Hawaii with my family. It is a powerful valley and one of my favorite places. I was enjoying listening to the ocean and was sitting on an old tree trunk when I felt the need to lay down.

Laying on the tree, I looked up at the sky and it was clear and sunny except for two wispy clouds. I began pondering spaceships and how they hide themselves with clouds. These tiny clouds were barely there and then I see a cigar shaped ship moving quickly through the sky. I watched it wondering if this was some kind of plane or something, but it had no wings.

It moved quickly and I had the memory pop in of Penny Kelly telling someone that there are cigar ships sometimes used to keep people in and to keep them safe for a later time while in stasis. I got so sleepy and fell asleep in total peace after this ship went out of my site.

Later that night, a friend sent me a YouTube from Elizabeth Klarer's documentary from *Beyond the Light Barrier* where she talks about the Venusian Mother Ships being cigar shaped! I knew exactly who was contacting me again as my hair stood on end!

Where is Andromeda?
Can we see it?
Who are the Andromedans?
Did they seed this planet?

Why are they contacting us?
Are they benevolent?
What do they look like?

The Andromeda Galaxy is 2.5 million light years away. I first learned of the Andromedans when I came to the Big Island of Hawaii for the first time to swim with wild dolphins. I was in my hotel room and it was late at night. Standing on the balcony, something kept drawing me into this one star in the night's sky.

This star was mesmerizing as I stared at it. I telepathed to the star and asked who it was. I heard clearly in my head, "Andromeda." I sat with this for a moment and felt the loving frequencies coming from Andromeda. I had never heard of it and it felt like they were letting me know who they were.

The next day after our swim with the wild dolphins, I attended a lecture given by Joan Ocean and she mentioned Andromeda. My ears perked up and I was shocked that she mentioned them. She began to say that the Andromeda Galaxy is coming towards our galaxy and they will eventually unite or merge with us. The Andromedan beings are making contact with humans who are ready.

I was surprised, yet this all made sense with what happened last night. Later, we did a meditation by the fire and I ended up in an Andromedan spaceship above her ranch. I could see these very tall beings with dark purple capes and they had what looked like collars to me. They were beaming light, had beautiful eyes, and their heads were bald.

The spaceship was large and expansive. I was led into a room where I laid down and I knew I was getting some type of healing. They used tones and music to heal me. It all felt very loving and guided. Andromedans are very advanced. Eventually, I came back down to Earth and I felt great.

Later, Joan mentioned that the Andromedans asked to have one of their spaceships above her ranch which she readily agreed. Anyone can ask to go into their ship for a healing. One time, I was at another meditation with Joan and a group, where we went on an Andromedan ship. When the meditation was over, a woman exclaimed that she was healed! She talked about how she couldn't move her neck and her back was in so much pain. After being with the Andromedans, she was completely healed!

I have found over the years of knowing the Andromedans, they are helping humans to heal and giving us healing technology. I have seen them while using certain types of frequency technologies to assist us. Some of these technologies where I have seen them are Trifinity 8 and Ascension 11 which are amazingly powerful. Dr. Kathy Forti was given the information on how to make these healing frequencies with crystals and many people have had incredible results.

Other times that I have seen the Andromedans, I have been meditating or sometimes I will be woken up by the Andromedans who come in and I seem to always go into their ships. It feels sometimes like they are adjusting my frequencies and turning on certain parts of my brain.

The Andromedans are one of the advanced civilizations of humanoids who have helped to seed planet Earth. They are here now helping us to make the leap in consciousness as this paradigm shifts. Those humans who feel ready to make contact with the Andromedans need only to ask and put their intent out there.

Some of you may have heard about The Andromeda Council which is made up from elders with many different planetary and galactic networks not just from Andromeda, but all over the universe. They are working together with many to bring peace and harmony to the cosmos.

Where is Lyra?
Who are the Lyrans?
Are they currently helping us?

What do they look like?
Are feline beings from Lyra?
Is this where humanoids first came from?

Lyrans are from the constellation of Lyra which is 206 million light years away from our sun. The Vega star is the brightest star in the galaxy and the fourth brightest star that we can see from Earth. Their constellation borders the Draco constellation. Lyra is close to the Galactic center or the Great Central Sun, Alcyone, when humanoids were first seeded.

Lyra is the considered the "cradle of life" in the Milky Way Galaxy which first seeded humanoid life as it was birthed from the Andromedan Galaxy. I have heard they are over ten billion years old. The Lyrians are our cosmic human ancestors who are the ancestral line of all humanoids in the galaxy according to some.

This constellation is also connected to the feline and avian beings. I had an experience at a seminar where I had past connections to a man there who was from Lyra. It was interesting as I had a love/hate pull towards this individual. He was absolutely gorgeous physically and was wearing a dress when I first saw him. Something inside me drew me to him and repulsed me at the same time.

The seminar continued for three days. On the second day, I found him in my hotel room with my roommate and it turned out that they knew each other. Then, during a class, he ended up sitting next to me and we began joking around. There was something so familiar about him.

After the class, we were talking in a hallway and I was looking into his eyes when he began to shapeshift right in front of me (this happens to me sometimes where I can see people's multidimensional selves). He was turning into a feline being and all my memories with him came back! I said to him, "I know you. I mean, I really know you!"

He responded, "What do you see?"

"You were a cat being in Egypt! You were a cat goddess! I was a dog being (felt like I was from Sirius) and we protected you. We were lovers. Then, you left! All of you just left us in Egypt!" I said quite upset.

He looked at me lovingly saying, "We were the feline beings from Lyra and we had to leave as the Earth was turning dark and dense. We chose not to participate in this, but we are back now!"

This was an incredible experience and my whole being resonated with truth and tears. We talked much more and I could feel the androgenous being he was as many Galactics are…a perfect balance of male and female. He was here incarnating to bring the sacred feminine back onto Earth spreading love, joy, bliss, and fun.

There are others I know who are of the Lyrans and have found them to be bringing in the sacred feminine energies back onto Earth at this time to bring balance. The "Mother Mary" energies are deeply connected to Lyra. Atlantis and Egypt have been connected with Lyra as well as the goddess Sekmet from Egypt who is a lioness humanoid and quite powerful. She is also connected to Sirius and maybe went through a portal there?

Just like all of our galaxies, Lyra also had wars as they evolved and expanded out in the galaxy. They warred with the Dracos, but have moved past these eons ago.

Some of you may have heard of the black panther beings? They are a very powerful group of beings who have been linked to Lyra and know how to jump dimensions and shapeshift. They are here on Earth now and have been, yet I don't know them well. I have been asking to connect with them more and have seen them when I have been time jumping. There is something so familiar about them to me. I am curious if the movie, *Black Panther*, was showing us more about the black panther beings as many movies are often ways of showing us truth.

Other feline beings from Lyra that are here are the jaguar beings that have been connected to the Amazon and the shamanic traditions. These are very powerful beings as well. The "big" cats are so present on our planet and many of us have connections to them. If you see them in your dreams, it often means that you are expanding your consciousness more, yet you could have close connections with Lyra. There are also the lion beings, but we will talk more about them with Sirius.

The smaller cats who we call our pets are very aware and are part of the collective who agreed to help us humans evolve by living with us just like dogs. They can see and hear things that we don't in other dimensions and you know this if one lives with you!

Where is Sirius?
Who are the Sirians?
Why are some sacred sites lined up with Sirius?

Is it a portal?
Have they helped us evolve?
What civilizations have had contact with them?

Sirius is sometimes called the "sun behind the sun" as it is twenty times the brightness of our sun. It is 8.6 light years away from Earth. Some people believe that our solar system orbits Sirius and not Alcyone (the great central sun). Many do still believe that our solar system and Alcyone orbit the galactic core of our Milky Way Galaxy which takes 225 million years to complete.

Time to travel in our spaceships to know for sure!

Sirius is the brightest star in our night's sky and is of the Canis Major constellation. You may also hear it called the "dog star" or Sothis. The Sirians are from the star system, Sirius, which is a triple star system and have planets labeled by our astronomers called Sirius A, B, and C. They are one of the original groups who seeded our Earth this time around.

The Sirians have made contact with many people throughout the world including our governments and other earlier civilizations like Egypt, Sumeria, Japan, Greece, and Wales. The Polynesians used Sirius to navigate by. The Egyptian calendar was based on the helical rising of Sirius. Sirians have also made contact with a group of people on our planet called the Dogons.

Some authors, like Robert M. Schoch, argue that the Dogons were a people who originated in Africa, but had to leave Egypt. The Dogons talk freely about their cosmic connections and that beings from the cosmos traveled on an "ark" (spaceship) that shot out fire and thunder, interacted with them giving them lots of information including that they were from a world that circled Sirius A.

French anthropologists, Marcel Griaule and Germaine Dieterlen, from 1931 to 1956 had many conversations with the Dogons to find out much of this information. Apparently, the sky God Amma is said to have created the first living creatures known as the "Nommo."

Shortly after Amma created the first "Nommo," the being transformed and multiplied into four pairs of twins. One of these twins rebelled against Amma and to restore the universal order, bringing peace once again, one of these "Nommo" were sacrificed. Its body was dismembered and scattered throughout the universe.

Does this sound familiar to anyone that knows Egyptian history around Isis and Osiris?

Fascinating.

The Dogons have drawn these "Sirians" which look like air-breathing fish from the oceans and some think they are dolphins because of their tail. The Dogons called them "Nommo" as a collective name. There are four different classes of "Nommos" according to the Dogons. These "Nommos" are masters of the water (perhaps the cosmos?).

"Nommos" had blue skin which seems to be related to other blue-skinned gods of the Vedas, Northern Japan, and Wales. They gave them much information and even gave them their location in the stars. The Sirians helped them advance and visited them from time to time.

Do you want to know something wild?

The Dogons pinpointed exactly where the planets of Sirius are and the rotation of them! Our scientists did not figure out the rotation of the planets in Sirius until 1970s! It doesn't stop here as the Dogons also knew of our planets in our solar system rotating around our sun as well as Saturn's rings and Jupiter's moons. Their calendars are based on Sirius, our sun, and Venus.

Recently, it has been shown that our solar system is not static in the cosmos, but is spiraling like a vortex through the cosmos, pulling the planets along with our sun as we orbit it.

The Dogons also shared that our sun is a "brother system" of Sirius. They say they got separated to form two different star systems, but of one identical origin. They also said that Sirius is the "eye of the world where they receive all knowledge."

In the documentary, *The Secret Life of Plants* which is a fascinating movie about how our plants feel, are conscious, and are connected to the cosmos as well, the Dogons said, "The seed and the star are the self-same substance, elements of a single universal consciousness."

Fascinating!
We are made of the stars.
We are universal consciousness.
We are made of "God stuff."

The Dogons celebrate the fifty year rotation of Sirius B (PoTolo) around Sirius A which recently happened in 2017, but they will not celebrate it until 2027. They say this rotation every fifty years is to renew our Earth as Sirius A seeds all life. The Dogons also said in *The Secret Life of Plants*, "The star (Sirius A) is the germinating seed sending out its shoots that are the creation of all life on Earth and all life throughout the universe."

Is Sirius the sun behind our sun? Does all energy coming into and out of our universe go through the portal of Sirius? It seems many ETs have travelled through Sirius to get to our solar system. What did our ancestors and the Dogons know?

It is important to note that often beings from the cosmos were depicted as being amphibious, as a fish with legs, or in water. Our ocean is like the cosmos and this is how ancient cultures depicted those from the cosmos. We have only explored one percent of our oceans, but if we knew more, we would know more about the cosmos and our origins.

Some of the interactions I have had with the Sirians are feeling them in ships under the water when I am out swimming with the dolphins. It has only happened a few times. There is a deep knowing and I can feel them below. I also hear the words, "Sirians" when I feel them.

More recently, I woke up one night and need to go to the bathroom. As I walked to the bathroom, something drew me to look out at the ocean. I could see a green light out there and again heard, "Sirian ship." I walked back to the bathroom and when I was finished, I came back to look out at the ocean. Mind you, we are up at two thousand feet in elevation and have a vast view of the ocean.

I saw another green light to the right of the other and I knew it was two Sirian ships out there. I watched for a while and went back to bed. Asking within myself if they were the ones that woke me up, I got a distinctive, "Yes."

My body was buzzing and I decided to sit up and meditate in bed as there was so much energy. I immediately felt the Sirians begin to tell me all about themselves. They look amphibious to me and they had gills on the sides of their necks. I perceived a small dorsal fin on the small of their spines.

They began to tell me that they live here on Earth in the water and go back and forth to Sirius through portals. They typically live in the oceans and have large cities underwater. It reminded me of the cities I have seen in my dreams, but also like in the movie, *Aquaman*.

I felt a kinship with them and reminded me of the games I used to play with my dad and brother as a kid pretending that we were all water beings. My dad was Aquaman, my brother was Aqui, and I was Aqualon. I loved remembering my underwater lives.

Anyways, the Sirians tell me that they are very into technology and that many are benevolent. It is just like any culture where some of the civilization are not. They are here helping to evolve this planet and there are some hybrids here on land as well. They also tell me that I am correct when I have felt them before.

As I sit with them, I also see them as these blue-type beings like in the movie, *Avatar*, that go in and out of the water. I am reminded of a life where I was in their civilization going in and out of the water on Earth to help other indigenous civilizations. They are very good shapeshifters.

The Sirians reminded me of the Dogons once again and also about them being in Egyptian times. Isis and Osiris were considered Sirius A and B to the Egyptians. Sirius was an important star to the Egyptians and they based their calendars upon the rising of Sirius just before our sun rose. The Great Pyramid of Giza in Egypt and other temples were lined up with Sirius when it rose to directly shine on the inner sanctum of the temples from millions of miles away in space. Was this the Egyptians connecting with their "gods" of Sirius?

The Great Pyramid of Giza was used as a time capsule, astronomical observatory, and initiation chamber. It was not a burial chamber as we have been led to believe. The Great Pyramid is made to resonate with sound and perhaps when it lined with Sirius, new resonances came onto our planet? Also, how did the Egyptians know that Sirius was the only fixed star with an unvaried cycle of 365.25 days? Perhaps it was the help from the Sirians?

Anyways, back to what the Sirians were showing me. They showed me how part of Sirius is a type of portal for beings to come here on Earth saying that the dolphin beings came through the portal of Sirius into our system. I can also see that mermaids and mermen are from the Sirius planet system. As I kept connecting with the Sirians, I heard the song, "Reunited" playing in my head and I could feel a deep love for this powerful star system.

The feline beings are very present on Sirius, yet I feel the lions beings more than other big cat beings like I have on Lyra. These lion beings are incredibly powerful and full of love from my experiences. Sekmet was an Egyptian goddess who was incredibly powerful and a lioness humanoid. I know them deeply and in my more recent meditations, I can see my multidimensional self as one of these Sirian lion beings. Their beautiful loving eyes meeting mine and seeing their mischievous tails moving like our cats here on Earth.

I know them.
I am them.
A reunion of deep connection with them.

The Sirians want humans to know about them and are very much part of the Galactic community of which humans are being invited. They remind me that I am one of the ET ambassadors helping to bridge the gap as we make our leap in consciousness.

There are also beings who call themselves "the Nine" or "Sirius Nine." This, to me, is similar to the group that Esther Hicks works with called "Abraham" who are helping to evolve our consciousness. I have two close friends who work with "the Nine" as their guides. I have seen this collective as well and they are a group of benevolent extraterrestrials here helping us evolve. I have worked with them at different times and feel the love and healing they have for us.

Sirius has also been linked to the occult with the Freemasons, Aleister Crowley, and Madam Blavatsky as well as the Viril society with Hitler. As with anything, we can use our powers for good or allow our power to be used for malevolent purposes. Did these people somehow learn the ways of the universe and use the power of Sirius for their own benefit? Was this their downfall?

Sirius and the Pleiades are very connected and it is said that the Pleiades is to Sirius as the Earth is to Venus. Sirians and Pleiadians are also connected to the dolphins and whales, so let's talk about them next!

What about the cetaceans?
Dolphins and whales?

They are technically "extraterrestrials!?"
They don't live on land!
Did they ever?
We have ETs right here!

Where did they come from?
Do they travel through portals under the ocean?
Are they multidimensional?
Are they telepathic?

Most of us love dolphins and whales and some of us go whale watching or swim with dolphins and whales. There is a bond between us and them that seems to go back eons. There are many stories of them saving humans or helping us. Many of us desire to swim with them because we respond to an inner coding which releases a new vibrational frequency as a result of our contact with dolphins. This frequency connects us with our right to know who we are.

Stephen Messenger wrote an article called *Dolphins and Humans are not so Dissimilar* in *the Dodo* in 2014, where he tells of David Busbee, a veterinarian from Texas A&M, who found that the human genome and dolphin genome were nearly identical. There are just a few chromosomal rearrangements. This makes total sense to me as we are not descendants from apes.

This will change how we view our history!

Cetaceans are extraterrestrials as they live in water and not on land. Joan Ocean, a researcher and scientist of cetaceans, was told this when she was looking for contact by ETs and her guides told her that she already was in contact with them. She was swimming with them every day!

According to Joan Ocean, dolphins came through a portal on Sirius into our reality system. The dolphins inserted themselves onto our timeline putting themselves backwards and forwards in time. They created their own history by putting themselves at different places in our history. They utilize portals in the oceans and have communication with spaceships in the ocean.

Simon Parkes, an ET contactee and whistleblower, also says that dolphins were brought here from one of the water worlds in the Sirius star system. He says that people here from Sirius and the Pleiades have a connection to the dolphins and water. Simon continues saying that Pleiadian people who were on Earth needed a body that had high resonance for their souls, so they merged with dolphins and whales. Those of us who are Sirian or Pleiadian in a human body will be drawn to dolphins and whales and will be recognized by dolphins and whales having telepathic communication with them in the oceans or at water parks.

Dolphins came in to help raise the frequency on this planet and to awaken humans. They are pure joy and most humans fall in love with dolphins. Remember the television show called *Flipper* in the 1980s?

Being multidimensional and telepathic, dolphins are here to teach us and remind us that we are as well. Not all dolphins came to interact with humans, but the Hawaiian spinner dolphins, bottlenose, and spotted dolphins sure did. Other dolphins have certain missions on this planet just like the pilot whales and false killer whales.

The whales in our oceans are the keepers of our history of this planet. They are wise beings and you can feel this when you are with them. The humpback whales sing new frequencies into this planet which are given from extraterrestrials like the Arcturians.

Joan Ocean, who has been with the cetaceans for over forty years, brought in much of the information about the whales and what they were doing. She even saw a spaceship on one of her trips to be with the whales where they were downloading new frequencies of information into the whales. Many others saw this as well.

There is just so much out there that we don't know about!

Whales also used to walk on land and there has been many bones found where they had legs. I wonder if they knew to get back into the oceans to keep themselves safe as the world was going to get crazy?!

I love being with the whales and there is just an energy and power to them. They are huge, gentle giants who are extraterrestrials right here on our planet. Whales are also telepathic and you can learn much from them. I have had the opportunity to be with the humpback whales, sperm whales, pilot whales, beaked whales, false killer whales, and others. When you are with them, you can feel their ET presence and intelligence.

When my son and I went to swim with the humpback whales in the Caribbean, we first got in with a mom and a baby whale. Mom stayed deep down and the baby would come up and down more as he needed to breathe more often. He came close to my son (who was eleven) and locked eyes with him.

Later, when we swam back to the boat, I asked my son what that was like for him. He replied, "Mom, my life will never be the same."

Talk about a mind-blowing experience!

I have swam many times with lots of types of dolphins especially the Hawaiian spinner dolphins. I have had some amazing experiences with them that I have detailed in my other book, *Fire and Water: Awakening the Dragon Within.* These dolphin beings are from another world for sure!

Humans are fascinated by dolphins and whales and there is a part of us that knows them. Some of us may be having other lives as them simultaneous as we are multidimensional or may have been them in a past or future life.

Dolphins and whales use sonar to move about the oceans and to scan what is out there as well as being able to heal others. There have been many accounts of people being healed after swimming with dolphins or that their consciousness began to expand more.

Some of my favorite cetaceans are the false killer whales. The first time I swam with them, I heard them when I was on the boat in the Caribbean. They sound like canaries in the sea to me. I was mesmerized by their sounds and couldn't get in the water fast enough.

When I did, I looked under our boat and there was one singing straight up into it. She then began to swim towards me as others came close too. I just floated in the sounds as they moved around me and I felt like I was in Heaven. There was something about these amazing beings that I long to be with again and again.

In Michael Roads book, *Journey into Nature*, he merged with a dolphin and said that dolphins learn by perception. Dolphins simply know by perceiving. They experience a number of identities in each life vs. the human, who usually experiences a single self in each life. Michael says, "Dolphins experience the individual in a shared basis thus, individuality is synthesized into a holistic experience. Oneness!" Dolphins share a perception of life which is experiencing without conclusions and this shared perception magnifies the experience.

Not knowing allows access to knowing.
No thinking allowed and clarity comes.
Allow what is to simply BE.

Where is Orion?
Can we see it?
Who are the Orions?
Did they seed this planet?

What are the Orion wars?
What do they look like?
Are they helping us?

The Orion constellation is 243 to 1300 light years away from Earth depending on which star you choose. Many people know of Orion as the "Orion's belt" and we can see it with our naked eye. If you follow it down, the belt leads to Sirius.

The Orions were seeded from the Lyrans and there is much controversary with this constellation. This has been a battleground of polarities as they are trying to evolve their consciousness, but have been infiltrated by the Dracos who have caused what some call, the "Orion Wars."

The Orion Wars are based on the movies, *Star Wars*, and many of us have been in the Orion system before which is why *Star Wars* was such a big hit. We all have some type of memories of being in these wars. These Orion wars were all about those in service to themselves instead of in service to others. They are very technologically advanced, but most are not spiritually.

The Orions are not all like this and many are benevolent just like other systems. Unfortunately, these wars moved to our planet Earth which is what we are in the middle of currently. It is truly a war on consciousness as we are trying to evolve and expand, taking a giant leap towards life!

There is also a slave trade throughout this system just as is depicted in the movies, *Star Wars*. Some humans have been kidnapped and sold in the cosmos to other systems. This may sound far-fetched, but this is what I have seen. Some of matrix of Orion has been able to trap and control astral bodies so that when you die, you are made to reincarnate into their system over and over. You can get out, but you must learn how.

I have not had much experience with beings from the Orion constellation, yet I know I have incarnated there before as I have memories of the wars there. These are humanoid beings and I know there are many benevolent ones trying to help their people. The Orion Council is working towards the good of the many.

Do we have other "extra"terrestrials on Earth?
Do some live inside the planet?
Is there light inside Earth?

How do you get inside the Earth?
Are there extinct animals living inside the Earth?

Do the tunnels below the Sphinx and Great Pyramid lead to the inner Earth?

Are there other points to enter the inner Earth?
What about the Kentucky caves?
What is Shamballa?
Agartha what?

Can ETs fly their spaceships through openings in mountains or just change their molecular structure or both to enter the inner Earth?

We have beings that are both from other galaxies here on Earth as well as having beings that live inside our Earth. Our planet is hollow and you can access the inner Earth by entering through the North or South poles. That being said, there are many other entrances to the Inner Earth and you can type that into a search on the computer for images of Inner Earth to see where many known entrances are...like under the Great Pyramid in Egypt.

Willis Emerson wrote a true story about the inner Earth in a book called *The Smoky God* where he describes what a man named Olaf told him about his experiences inside the inner Earth in the 1800s. He and his father were up towards Norway and beyond on a boat and somehow found the entrance through the North pole into the inner Earth.

They weren't looking for it, but they were in awe at what they found. The water was fresh water and they described it as a Garden of Eden. They were met by tall, benevolent human beings about twelve to fifteen feet in size who were singing on a boat. Their boats levitated and were like the land cruisers in the movie, *Star Wars*, but bigger.

Olaf and his father were then taken into their world where they saw animals that had been extinct for eons like Mammoths and Saber-toothed tigers. The trees and plants were giant and everything lived in harmony. The leaders of the inner Earth beings said that they were making contact with surface humans so that we knew there is more out there. This inner Earth paradise also had an inner sun which is why they called the book, *The Smoky God*.

The whole book resonated with me deeply and I could feel its truth. Olaf and his father eventually left the inner Earth and tried to get back to their Norway home, but they had to leave through the South pole which was dangerous. Olaf's father was killed and Olaf was rescued by a passing boat.

The story goes on to tell of how Olaf tried to tell people what he and his father experienced, but nobody believed him and they put him in jail for twenty years. Finally, when he got out, he moved to America in Los Angeles, California. Here, he kept his story to himself until his death bed where he told a close neighbor, Willis Emerson, the whole truth.

This isn't the only inner Earth story.

In the 1940s, Admiral Byrd was commissioned by the US military to fly a plane through the portal of the North pole into the inner Earth. He did and found the inner Earth beings. Admiral Byrd saw how beautiful everything was and came back with messages for us surface humans.

This was all kept secret from the world except that Admiral Byrd wrote it all down in his journal. He wanted to tell everyone, but was not allowed to because the military classified it. After he died, his journal was released by his family.

I have had close contact from Olaf from the other side and had other experiences of being in the inner Earth. It feels like a second home to me. There are other civilizations in the inner Earth referred to as the Agartha network and Shamballa is often referred to as a city there.

There are many mountains that are portals for ETs to come in and out of. Some of those are well known like Mt. Shasta in California and Mt. Adams in Washington. Both of these mountains have connections to the inner Earth civilizations. James Gilliland, who owns ECETI ranch near Mt. Adams, calls the inner Earth beings, "Elvin" beings and says that they have guarded the openings to the inner Earth.

At Mt. Shasta, there are beings from an inner Earth civilization called Telos where a being named Adama has communicated with some of us surface humans. These are said to be the ancient Lemurians who went into the inner Earth when Lemuria was sinking. There are some books that have been written about Adama of Telos and this inner Earth civilization. I first heard about inner Earth beings while reading a snowboarding magazine years ago. These snowboarders were snowboarding on Mt. Shasta with the hopes of meeting some of the inner Earth beings. Their trip was successful.

Antarctica is another place where our governments have been accessing the inner Earth and other advanced civilizations. There is much of the world's population that has been kept in the dark about ETs and the inner Earth, believing the Earth is solid. In fact, there are rumors that Adolf Hitler went into Antarctica and never truly died!

There are other beings on our planet who come here to live or vacation just as we would to another country. They go into the inner Earth and into underwater civilizations. They are telepathic and can read our minds to know when they should disappear if on the surface. Some of these beings are tall with white skin and blond hair.

According to some, the Paradise fires in California in 2017 were a direct attack from a secret, rogue government called "the cabal." Apparently, the benevolent ETs that lived there also had places underground and were getting ready to tell us that they existed. The dark (shadow) government did not like this and used their direct energy weapons (DEWs) to laser the city destroying everything with high intensity fires.

Are we not surprised that we literally have ETs living among us and within the Earth? Our religions and sciences teach us that the Earth is solid, yet even with the laws of physics, this doesn't make sense with how the Earth spins. Most planets are hollow and our moon is as well. Also, most extraterrestrials don't live on planets, but inside them as the surface may not be hospitable. So, they create their own environments which are amazing.

What about Bigfoot or Sasquatch?
Do they exist on Earth?
Are they from another star system?

What are they doing here?
What if they do exist?
Why don't they want us to see them?

I felt guided to put Bigfoot in this book even though they are very of the Earth, yet they also seem to have come from elsewhere. How did they get here and where are they from initially? These are still unanswered questions that I have myself.

The Sasquatch (aka Bigfoot and Yetis) work closely with the inner Earth beings as protectors of Mother Nature and are contacting humans who are benevolent to help our environment. They are part of the dimensional realm of fairies, divas, elves, leprechauns, and many others who are here protecting our Mother Earth.

These Sasquatch know how to shift their energy to become invisible to avoid confrontation just as the Hathors do. They know most of us humans are very unpredictable and want to capture them. So, they avoid most of us. The Sasquatch also know how to work with the portals on our planet from what I have seen of them.

I find it funny that I did not believe in the existence of Sasquatch even though I knew of other ET races. It was on the Big Island of Hawaii that their collective first came through for me. I was at Joan Ocean's ranch out in the woods when I woke up to feeling surrounded by loving Sasquatch. There was so much love and I began to deeply laugh as they were showing me how real they were. I felt they came through a portal there.

Anyways, from other experiences, I have found the Sasquatch to be so loving and gentle, too. I have had continued contact with them and know that I am to talk about them being real. In my book, *Fire and Water: Awakening the Dragon Within*, I tell more of my experiences with them. I have never seen one with my physical eyes, but with my third eye and through telepathy. They also have a great sense of humor.

The Sasquatch are lovers of Mother Nature and keepers of the Earth. They want to have contact with those of us in our hearts and to develop deep relationships with us again.

Are there other advanced beings out there?
What about the Mantis beings?
What about the Ant beings?
The insectoids?

Ever heard of the Golden Triangle beings?
Who are the tall white or Nordics?
And Avian beings?

If we can imagine it, it exists out there somewhere! This has been my experience and we forget how powerful our imagination is. Imagination is what creates reality through plasma physics and Source.

There are so many other beings that are not humanoid or human out there and I just wanted to bring that point to light. There are insectoid races and I have communicated some with the Praying Mantis beings. These beings are incredibly powerful in their consciousness. I don't know much about the other insectoid beings at the moment, but I am continually learning.

I do know that the Golden Triangle beings exist and have seen them only in some meditations. They have a Golden Triangle for a head. There are also tall whites and Nordics which sometimes get confused with Pleiadians. And there are lots of Avian beings from what I have seen that go way back.

Are all ETs benevolent?
Can some be malevolent?

If they are advanced races, wouldn't they all be benevolent?

How do you know?
Are there both here on Earth right now?

What do you do if some extraterrestrial is trying to tell you to do something that doesn't feel right?

Advanced extraterrestrials are not to directly interfere in the evolution of a planet which is why many starseeds directly incarnate here on Earth. You can become part of the reality system, but many of us forget why we came here. We can ask for help from the advanced ETs and they can help this way. We must be able to discern the different extraterrestrial energies as this is a free will universe and all forms of life are allowed here.

The way to tell the difference from the benevolent and malevolent beings is by how you feel in their presence. Get in touch with who you are and what feels good or not. The benevolent ones will never tell you to do something against yourself or to harm another. The dark ones will try to control you, frighten you, or manipulate you.

Don't go into fear. You are in a body, so you can tell them to leave. Your fear attracts them and instead, get into what makes you smile. Raise your vibration and get in your heart because you have a choice!

The Earth realm is in a battle right now of light and dark as the light is helping those of light and dark are helping those of dark. The dark don't want us to awaken our consciousness, yet by this contrast, it is pushing us to evolve our consciousness or die. Remember, just because someone has advanced technologies or magical abilities, it does not mean that they are advanced spiritually.

It is important to be kind and not to speak negatively when we speak of the dark forces. You may be thinking that this is crazy to think this way, but simply the dark forces are merely uninformed. They create systems based on fear that do not honor life because they are uninformed and have separated themselves from the knowledge of who they truly are. Send them nothing but love and light!

Here on Earth, the dark forces are mostly made up of the "Lizzies" as the Pleiadians call them. They are part human and part reptilian. There are some benevolent ones within these "Lizzies," yet many are malevolent feeding on chaos and fear. This is why the fear frequency is blasted to us by those elite who think they are in charge of the planet and are in love with power.

It is so important to have control over your own frequency and to not continually feed the fear frequency. Just as humans can be both benevolent and malevolent, so can other ET races. We need to trust ourselves and learn discernment to make decisions. Knowing within is our connection to Source and you can feel knowing within your body.

There is a lot talked about these days in regards to the Reptilians or "Lizzies." These are "feeder" beings who feed on fear and negative emotions of humans and other sentient beings. They love to generate conflict and chaos as this is more food for them. These "Lizzies" come from the Draco constellation. They invaded and came into the Orion Galaxy causing issues there as well. They are war like and the conquerors of worlds.

These "Lizzies" came onto Earth and manipulated the humans here through shutting off parts of our DNA thus creating humans to worship "godlike" beings with superpowers. "Lizzies" can shapeshift into humans disguising their reptilian features, yet some of us know when one is around us as "the hair on the back of your neck stands up."

The Anunnaki are talked about with the "Lizzies" and were snake/reptilian like which led many to believe that they are one in the same. They are ten to twelve feet tall, very powerful, and love to be worshipped. These were the beings who Zachari Sitchin talked about in his many books. There is talk that the Anunnaki were from planet Nibiru.

These Anunnaki were very advanced, but unevolved. The god of the Bible in the old testament is one of these gods who was jealous and wrathful. Enlil and Enki were Anunnaki who came here to Earth and were worshipped by humans. Enlil (or Jehovah) was this wrathful god while Enki had compassion for the humans. It was Enlil who created the flood on Earth to wipe out all of humanity while Enki warned Noah of the coming flood.

It is these "Lizzies" who have created intergalactic slave trade of humans both on and off planet and this is again portrayed well in the movies of *Star Wars*. These beings also worked with Hitler and the Viril society in exchange for advanced technology.

We have some of this Reptilian DNA within ourselves and many of us are working to not let the reptilian part of our brain take over. There is understanding it to move beyond it. There are some "Lizzies" that are here now that are trying to remedy their past mistakes of trying to control humans.

Some ET races have lost the ability to reproduce like the Greys and Zetas. They typically make babies within test tubes, petri dishes, or simulators. A hybrid is a way to strengthen your race and sometimes they are looking for our DNA.

The Zetas are from the Zeta Reticuli galaxy and don't have a great rap sheet. Many Greys are benevolent, but others not. Both of these are humanoids where they have this type of body suit, but are different than humans like in many of the galaxies that we have talked about. Many humans look like us, but may be different in height, different shapes, different heads, different eyes, or different metabolism. Some of them have made deals with our governments to extract DNA from us and other beings here. This is why some people talk about being abducted and are afraid of ETs.

Currently, we have benevolent and malevolent ones working with and within our governments throughout our planet. There is a huge undertaking with benevolent ETs and humans of exposing the malevolent beings within and "draining the swamp" as it has gotten deep with all the corruption, greed, and power. Malevolent humans have aligned with these malevolent ETs for their own power and greed using fear as their weapon.

It is fascinating that those in power are really after total control. They want total power as they want to only do things their way as they believe it is the best way. They have developed their technology, but not their consciousness. These races are evolving just as we all are.

Remember, this is a free will planet and we can tell the malevolent beings to get out and stop. They are helping us to get back into our power and start being the creator beings that we are. Pay attention to your beliefs and what you are feeding. Watch your emotions and your thoughts!

The "gods" are really humans who have developed their consciousness!

Get out of your head and out of fear as it is their favorite food. The dark forces love fear, anxiety, chaos, despondency, etc… The light forces food source is love.

Conquer your own fears and show the rest of the planet that there is nothing to fear! When you are in your heart space and blasting the frequency of love, it destroys them. Do not be afraid of their looks or their powers.

You are more powerful!

What about plants, insects, birds, reptiles, and animals?
Where did they come from?
Are they evolving like us?

Elves, Menehune, Leprechauns, little people?
Fairies, Divas, tree spirits?
Are they really here on Earth?
Are they evolving?

What about machines, the air, the ocean?
Are they listening?
What do they want to say?

I often feel that Mother Nature is so much more intelligent than we give her credit and much more intelligent than humans. Sometimes, I feel that animals and plants are more evolved than we are or perhaps they are just mirroring our behaviors back to us. They are already telepathic and have been waiting for us.

We evolve, they evolve.
Time for us to step up!

The beings of light can use animals and pets as instruments of instruction to help those starseeds on Earth. When we hold our animals, play with them, or they sleep next to us, we can be receiving special instructions from our ET friends or spirit mentors. We can be activated on our Earth mission.

The insects, birds, reptiles, and many animals all come from other galaxies as this Earth is truly a huge compilation of so many beings of many galaxies. The birds or avians came from Lyra constellation while the reptiles came from the Draco constellation. Many insectoids come from many galaxies. Some animals like the cat beings come from Lyra and Sirius.

These insects, birds, reptiles, animals, trees, plants, etc...all experience love and feel love because everything is consciousness. Everything. Love is not specific to humans as we may think. Love is embedded in the consciousness.

Talking to animals, plants, insects, etc… is important as it gets us to learn how to communicate with other ET beings. Animals and others are just in another frequency set and we can tune our brains into hearing them with intent and practice.

In the book, *Change We Must*, Nana says that the ancient Hawaiians knew how to work with the elements and a key component was to be humble. Her mother taught her that the plants have feelings and cry when you pull their leaves and flowers off, so always ask permission from the plant. This shows that you are acknowledging the spirit in all things and have a reverence for life. The ancient Hawaiians spoke with the plants, trees, ocean, and rocks, yet to hear them, you need listen as they are telepathic. Silence was an important part for them as it connected them to the "all-knowing center" which is the Source of our being.

How about the elf dimension? What are they? These are the intelligences that take care of our trees, flowers, fruits, vegetables, forests, and is part of Mother Nature. They present themselves as little people like elves, leprechauns, and Menehune.

They are amazing beings!

The divas and fairies are the spirits that take care of our elements, plants, and food. We can talk with them and ask them to help us with gardening and growing food. We also need to remember that we need to leave parts of the land natural, so the elf beings can thrive. We humans think it looks like chaos, but this is the nature of Mother Nature.

Remember, we are not the only ones creating on this planet. We need to remember that there are other dimensions here and not just those from the stars. The Elf dimension used to live on the surface of the Earth. Now, they have lived for tens of thousands of years underground because humans dropped in consciousness and stopped talking to them. They went underground to avoid being attacked, persecuted, and captured by humans.

Elves are small and have pointy ears, but they take on any form. They are very wise and every continent has them. In Ireland, Leprechauns are seen regularly as well as the Menehune in Hawaii. There are lots of stories about the Menehune helping the Hawaiians and they can be mischievous, too. They just exist in a different frequency zone.

If you really want to deeply understand Mother Nature, ask to study and learn from the Elf dimension. It is their specialty. You can learn about the elemental forces, soil, trees, plants, insects, and animals. You can do this in dreamtime or during waking consciousness.

The elementals are very alive and conscious. They are always listening and are the forces of nature like the wind, fire, water, metal, and Earth. I have had many conversations with all of these as well as our Sun who all have much to teach us. They really want to have a relationship with us.

The wind and rain love to know what we want and need. The fire is assisting on burning up old energies, but needs to know what we need as well. Metal was an interesting one for me as I didn't think inanimate objects had consciousness for a long time. I learned that they have lots to say and I have a fun relationship with my appliances especially my washer and dryer.

I have been playing with merging my consciousness with many things and it has been fun to merge myself with my washer and dryer whom I call Whirl and Tromm from Whirlpool and LG Tromm. When I drive my car, I have been expanding myself into my car and becoming one with it. When it happens, I see my face on the front grill of my car. I think I am falling in love with all of Mother Nature…really all of life!

I feel this is how we make conscious spaceships. We merge our energy with theirs and become one. Are you ready to jump to this level of consciousness?

I AM!

I had a conversation with a stone wall once who showed me how they are the structure of the Earth like the bones of our bodies. They give structure to our reality and nutrients to all plants, animals, and humans. You can merge with them by viewing the rock as energy rather than a stone. Then, allow that energy to access your being.

Mother Nature is waiting for us to come back to the conversation, so that she can share her secrets with us for within humanity, is the whole of nature. The physical world can only reveal so much, but going into Mother Nature is where we find a deeper understanding. We need to evolve both our consciousness and technology with Mother Nature. Look at how much of our technology copies Mother Nature like our airplanes, submarines, and weapons.

Are we done copying Mother Nature for the purpose of killing each other? Can you imagine what our world would be like without war? We could jump ahead eons in consciousness if we would evolve our consciousness.

Some of our insect friends, especially the bees and ants, live together in large numbers and work together for the common good of all.

Can we humans copy this instead?
If we choose to!

PART THREE:

MORE MIND-EXPANDING TOPICS

Are there new energies besides Newtonian physics?
Are you ready to learn about them?
Do scientists consider the role of consciousness?

Ever heard of plasma physics?
What about Dr. Levengood or Mehran Keshe?
Are you ready to expand your consciousness?
Does it matter what we think and say?

What if this new energy would create a whole new world?

Scientists have been struggling to figure out where consciousness fits into the world of science. Most scientists discard consciousness as they believe that it can't be measured, but can it? What happens when someone dies and leaves the body? You only need to be out of the body one time to know that consciousness does not die when the body dies for we are a field of consciousness!

Ever had an OBE (out of body experience)? You can come and go from your body while your body is still alive and see for yourself. Robert Monroe had a spontaneous OBE and began investigating what this was all about in the 1960s and beyond. He started the Monroe Institute where you can learn to have an OBE and much more. We create in many realities with or without a body.

Perhaps we need to change our terminology and integrate consciousness into science to help us make this leap in consciousness? Science is incredibly important in the advanced ET races as is consciousness. We need both as they both complement each other.

Let's see what we can agree on. Scientists agree that we have space and as space begins to move, we call that energy. As energy compresses, it becomes a particle where they exist or wink out. How does this translate into the world of plasma physics?

With plasma physics, let's look at Penny Kelly's information that she was given by Source to get a foundation as consciousness goes with these stages of formless to form. You can find this in her books or videos on Patreon and YouTube.

So, the first stage is mind/space which is called Source in the metaphysical world, God in the religious world, or space in the science world. This is the original Source material from which we are all made of. In ancient times, it was known as the Void, I AM, or the oneness state. It is pure bliss, silence, and peace. There is nothing here except pinpoint-sized lights and awareness. This is exactly what Esther Hicks saw when she first began conversing with the beings known as "Abraham" when she asked "Abraham" to show themselves…infinite amounts of tiny lights.

Space is alive and is the location aspect of mind. Mind is the awareness aspect of space. Now, as mind/space begins to move (I am curious as to why it does, as why leave pure bliss?!), the next state it becomes is consciousness and energy. Energy is the motion of consciousness and consciousness is the feeling aspect of energy. If motion changes, feeling changes.

Here is a little secret...this energy has unlimited potential if you know how to use your consciousness and direct it. This can also be known as "the Force." Energy is the ability to do work and sounds like a roaring to those who have had a kundalini experience. This consciousness and energy moves next into the state of intelligence and particles which still retain the qualities of mind/space and consciousness/energy.

A particle is a communication center and the intelligence is the ability to cooperate. It is communicating its location, spin, motion, charge, etc... The next transition or state is when the particles become a pattern with the intention to maintain this pattern. The intent is the awareness, consciousness, and intelligence to keep this pattern, shape, and function. This is what makes up our reality system.

Now, let's discuss plasma which is how things get created in the physical as form. We need to understand plasma to make a leap in consciousness as it opens doorways to new understandings and technologies.

Plasma is a magnetic field that holds various kinds of particles in it. These plasmas are currents of energy that collect into particles and arrange themselves into patterns which become a three-dimensional physical form. Understanding plasma is important because both individual and collective consciousness produces matter (form) and plasma teaches us the science behind such terms as, "our thoughts create our reality," "why we attract what is around us," and why it is important to "Know Thyself."

Plasma is the basis for creating everything and with this, there is truly no lack as it all comes from plasma currents which come from space. Space is not empty, but loaded with frequencies. Plasma is the formless energy that becomes form!

Plasma physics is a new type of science that has been around since the late eighteen hundreds developed by Kristian Birkeland. In the early nineteen hundreds, Hannes Alfven continued the plasma revolution. Birkeland said that the Earth's aurora is electric and that space is filled with plasma. Alfven said that there was no "big bang" and actually created the concept of plasma physics.

Other scientists like William Levengood, Gerald Pollack, Mehran Keshe, and Wallace Thornhill have deeply explored plasma physics and they know this is the basis for free energy, anti-gravity, changing the nature of matter, the electric universe, and our electric sun.

Nikola Tesla, who was a brilliant scientist, inventor, and also a Venusian, knew about plasma physics. He said that, "Earth is a Tesla coil" and that "electromagnetic levitation disproves gravity." Nikola figured out high speed space drives, yet our scientists chose the route of explosion motors. Plasma physics actually validates some of his work and his work was stolen by the government. It was classified after he died. Trump's uncle actually worked with Tesla and had access to his information.

At *safireproject.com*, plasma physics is already being used in our world to generate energy, produce heat, produce rare Earth elements, and to neutralize radiation. This would shift our 450 nuclear power plants that we have around the world by rearranging the particles from the radiation waste, making them neutral. Plasma physics is bringing us one step closer to becoming ageless, time travel, teleporting, instant manifestation, shapeshifting, and space travel!

Is it possible that plasma teaches us about teleporting because teleportation utilizes the phenomenon of going back and forth from mind/space to the patterns of a human? You could also say this a different way as from form to formless and formless to form in another location. Also, technically speaking, you could say this again another way...from matter to GANS to plasma back to GANS to matter. The consciousness has moved from one space to another in a very fluid process.

GANS is a new state of matter and is an abbreviation for gas to nano (expanded state) to solid where a molecule of gas becomes a nano itself, appearing as a solid state of matter. Each GANS acts as a small sun radiating energy outwards and receiving energy, emitting stronger fields than any other matter state. These nano states are expanded fields of its form which is really an expanded consciousness. This is important because you can take in more energy and see expanded perspectives. This is just what kundalini does to we humans by expanding our human potential, taking in more energy and expanding our consciousness.

To put this in an everyday perspective, this is the same thing that happens in our bodies when we eat food (matter). It transforms into GANS (breakdown of food) then to pure plasma (needed electromagnetic frequencies) where our cells take in what they need. Then, the plasma goes back to GANS (waste products) to excrement (matter). This is why it is important to eat nutritional foods as our body is made up of millions of plasma fields!

Our bodies are plasma in the GANS state of matter and every organ in our bodies is made up of GANS which use different energy fields according to Mehran Keshe. We actually take in about 80% of what we need from the environment (plasma fields) around us through our skin and breath, and only 20% from food. Plasma physics is leading the way to allow us to restore the body to its original healthy state as needed as it is all about the frequencies.

Most ETs eat a nutritional paste to take in certain frequencies according to Penny Kelly. You can also bring in energies from Source by getting quiet, breathing in, and letting down your boundaries for a moment. We are an energy system with boundaries. Let your boundaries down for a moment and let the Source just fill you up. You can target certain parts of your body and allow Source to fill up certain parts that hurt. I like to do this with the Sun's energy as well. You can also merge with your car and see how it is running if there is an issue by letting down your boundaries.

Breatharians are taking in energies directly from the energies around them…Source. They often bring it in through the eyes and then they anchor the energy by walking barefoot on the ground for an hour. Do this for a year or so and you never need to eat again.

Creating food (energy) right out of thin air!
We continually absorb and emit plasma fields.

Mehran Keshe said that blackholes are the "mother feeding of universal energy." This is pure plasma energy. Lightning and pictures of fractals are pure plasma energy that we can see with our eyes coming into form. Mehran Keshe also said, "Plasma is a house of fields that responds directly to our consciousness." So, as we put our attention on anything, plasma, which carries electrical currents creating a magnetic field, will cause it to manifest in our physical dimension.

Everything is alive and listening.
Everything is consciousness.

Everything is plasma within this electric and magnetic universe. Plasma is usually made up of red, blues, and greens. Our thoughts are conscious and plasma begins to form around them as we think them over and over again until we have it manifested in the physical. Plasma currents are all around us. We are electrical beings and are an electric universe!

It is known among advanced races that there are many types of light and they are all moving at different rates of speed. Light comes from the interaction and friction of plasma fields which our eyes can see, yet there is still much we don't see as the world is in constant motion.

Dark matter or dark energy is very dense light moving at high rates of frequencies. It is light that moves so high that it is almost solid and looks dark. We can't really see it, so it looks dark to us. Human speech and thought convert dark energy into plasma! Words that come out of our mouth are sound or frequency which impacts the Source creating dynamic forms becoming plasma which become physical form.

Undisciplined thoughts and speech mess up the fields of frequency. It is like trash and you create what you don't want. This is why many advanced races don't speak unless they know exactly what they want to create for thought is a vibration and therefore, a force. Thought is energy and the creative medium of our reality. To think is to create and when you add feelings along with it, it manifests quickly in the physical.

Become aware of your thoughts.
They are powerful.

Our mind is incredibly powerful, yet we don't realize it and create so much of what we don't want. We are receiving and emitting plasma continuously which impacts everyone around us with our plasma fields and many of us are aware of someone's positive or negative energy (plasma field). We can feel it because it begins to interact with ours!

If you find yourself repeating the same negative issues in your life, it is because your plasma field is attracting the same plasma fields and patterns to you, creating more layers of the same negative emotions. Become aware of what you are putting out there as what we give out, comes back, creating a feedback loop. Clearing old emotional patterns will attract different plasma fields to you for a field of happiness, creates happiness around us or a field of fear, creates fear around us.

"You form the fabric of your experience through your own beliefs and expectation," according to Jane Roberts who wrote and channeled the *Seth Book: The Nature of Reality*. She goes on to say, "Your beliefs can be like fences that surround you. The self is not limited. There are no boundaries or separations of the self." Are you ready to start taking responsibility for what you believe? This is creating your reality.

You are an amplifier of the plasma fields others give you. Are you inadvertently amplifying negativity and fear? You choose what you accept from others. Shift any negative thoughts by becoming aware of them and choosing a positive thought.

Plasma physics shows that more negative thoughts will be attracted if we don't catch it right away. One easy way to shift this quickly is by moving into an attitude of gratitude or visualize something that makes you happy. If the thoughts have progressed to emotions before you become aware of this "snowball," feel the emotions and become the observer of them (no attachment). Allow them to move through and transform.

Become a Master of Energy.

"If we can change our plasma fields, we can change our frequencies, we can change our patterns, we can change our health, we can change our life. It is that simple," according to Penny Kelly in her online Patreon plasma class.

Most humans don't realize how powerful we are and generally speak things that we don't want. We put our attention on things we don't want and then we create it not realizing how this world works. Advanced extraterrestrials don't speak or telepath unless they know what they want to create. They know how powerful their words and intentions are.

We can manifest anything that we want if we know how to arrange the frequency matrix and set up the waves that then become fields that hold the plasma that then become matter. This is the true definition of abundance...to create what you need any time you need it. Can you imagine this? Do you remember your lives on other planets where you did this?!

Let's create this now!

Mehran Keshe has released all his plasma physics information/blueprints to the world for free and how it works from a scientific perspective. He put the blueprints online on how to build his "Magrav power unit" (plasma generator) that any of us can build including the healing GANS technology. This can be used to help us get off grid and heal ourselves. People are also experimenting with creating plasma fields with these units to create conscious spaceships and plasma fields for instant manifestation.

Just go to *keshefoundation.org* to learn more.
This is the next step to a "no money" society!
Plasma physics is spaceship science.

Plasma becomes matter or form through consciousness. Everything is listening. Watch your thoughts and words for not one thought is ever lost. Life is a system and needs to be maintained by all of us.

It is important to note that plasma is always looking for ways that it can organize itself at a higher level of function. Everything wants to bring a better world! You are made of this God stuff (mind/space) and you can talk to it making it what you want. Everything is made from plasma fields and is connected to the Source (creator), therefore we are the creator as nothing is separate as we are taught to believe.

What are you creating with "the Force" around you?

What if time isn't real?
Is time real?

Why does time not exist in other dimensions?
Or does it?
What does "timeless" mean?
What really is time?
Is it all about frequencies?
What is time/space?

Why do things take "time" here on Earth?
How do we step "out of time?"
Does it have anything to do with our perception?

What about timelines and time travel?
Is this even real?

We measure time with the rotations of the Earth around the sun to get 365.25 days in a year based on the position of the Earth in space. Time is a mental structure to divide the day and night. Our Earth spins giving us the appearance of day and night with twenty-four hours in a day. We have equinoxes and solstices (also known as seasons) based on the tilt of the Earth.

We also have what our scientists call time/space here where space is loaded with frequencies as we just talked about with plasma physics. Space is not empty! Time/space is really a reality zone which on Earth is our reality system. Within our reality zone, there can be many systems of reality, but they are all related. Let's go deeper into time and what it is from another perspective.

Time is the rate at which perception moves from one form or one center of action to another according to Penny Kelly. Time is frequency plus perception. So, the rate at which you move your perception from one frequency to the next is the determinate of time. If you move your perception in a slow manner, time is slow. If you move your perception frantically, time speeds up.

Simple, right?

Now, continuing with Penny Kelly's interpretation of time, within space or a specific location, you have a range of frequencies all working together and all synchronized harmoniously to one another. This is what determines the rate at which we experience time (our perception). Continuing on these lines, if you stop moving your perception completely while focusing totally on one thing, time will stop. Ever had that happen? You may have had that happen with something shocking that happened to you, perhaps a life or death situation. People in accidents often describe time going in slow motion or stopping.

A friend of mine, Joan Ocean, told me how she actually experienced time stopping and standing still. She was in a new age type store in San Diego in the 1980s. Joan was with a friend and looking at a John Lily book when she noticed the music coming over the speakers. She didn't really like it, so she moved her perception out of it. A few minutes later, Joan looked up after she heard a tone from the music and everyone in the store had frozen…they literally stopped moving and were frozen in their positions!

Joan looked around and even her friend was frozen while flipping a page. The cashier was handing someone money and was frozen with her hand out. Joan didn't understand what was happening, but the music in the store was still playing!

Then, another tone went off in the music. Suddenly, everyone began to be animated again! Try to wrap your head around that one!

It is all about frequency.
Was something being reset?
How often does this happen?

When you are in a time band like Earth, typically, you have slow frequency and slow perception. As you expand your consciousness, your perception increases faster and faster and you move beyond time. You enter the "timeless" frequency. The added benefit of this is that you also know much more. "Timeless" frequencies are simply another type of time that is moving at a different frequency rate having different rules, results, and effects.

When you are out of this Earth based time frequency and in a higher frequency, things will happen quicker as they are "timeless." Things happen in a way that is dependent on your own perception. Increase your own frequency and you can perceive more reality zones. You can move your perception from this Earth reality where "time" moves slowly into another reality system where "time" is moving faster. Weeks and months could pass in the other system versus only twenty minutes may have passed here on Earth.

Wild!

Time is also personal, not universal. It can expand and contract. Time stops when your perception stops. Dan Winter in his book, *Fractal Conjugate Space and Time*, expands on this as well saying that "time can stretch and compress according to our state of consciousness." Just look at your dreams and how much information is included in seconds or when receiving information from the cosmos. It can happen instantly. In an expanded state of consciousness, it takes no time to go anywhere as we are omnipresent.

You want to heal your fears, worries, traumas, and biases because they will create situations that you don't want and get in the way as things, conditions, and situations materialize much faster. We get a taste of what it is to be in some of the high frequencies when we enter a dream that is extremely real and then proceeds in a clear and somewhat logical manner. This is why lucid dreaming is so powerful and we can make things happen.

The ability to move time is simply the ability of tweaking a particular frequency set in a particular location. If you change the frequency set, you change time.

We are moving past time.
We are coming to the end of time!
Time is malleable.

We don't need to try and change an event, but to change the self. We need to change the inner self. The frequency location can stay the same, but we aren't attracted to it! Our energy frequency has totally shifted.

Imagine that!

In the book, *Beyond the Light Barrier*, the Alpha Centaurians talk about how the wave motion of light controls the destiny of humans with "its pulse wave creating the vast and everlasting waves of the oceans." This energy spirals and varying frequencies give us the nature of existence in matter and antimatter which create planets, stars, and people in varying frequencies of time. We can see this wave motion of light when an earthquake moves across the land.

Knowing is part of the "timeless" realms as well as seeing the "big picture." Telepathy is also inherent in the "timeless" frequency bands as telepathy is instantaneous. When you are telepathic, you experience others' thoughts as they think it.

Ever experience that?

Telepathy can happen in an instant outside of time and it can still happen here on Earth, yet it can be challenging because the consciousness is slow. There is often lots of noise going on around you and the message can get lost between the sender and receiver unless you are focused. You can practice telepathy with plants and animals as they are very receptive. We just need to listen.

Ever wonder what they have to say? Can you imagine that everything is listening and has a consciousness? Ever read *The Secret Life of Plants* by Peter Tompkins or watched the documentary?

Plants feel and are intelligent.

So, being timeless also goes hand in hand with being an eternal being. When you enter a timeless place and can manipulate all the frequencies, plasma currents, and plasma fields, you can live forever. This is actually our birthright and all we need do is to let go of fear and doubt which is a man-made illusion. We do this by staying in constant connection to the Source within ourselves. Source will meet you there if you make the leap. You realize that your body is eternally beautiful, pure, and perfect. You are an eternal being.

In the book, *Life and Teachings of the Masters of the Far East* by Baird Spalding, he met many masters who were immortal and were hundreds to thousands of years old. They knew how to keep their physical body ageless and work with Source assisting many on Earth. These masters understood plasma physics and could manifest anything directly from the space around them, coming and going as they pleased. They were showing Baird Spalding and his group that we could also do these things if we choose.

Is this our goal...to become an eternal being?
Death is a mistake in thinking.

Penny Kelly also says that our goal is to become an eternal being and that we need to talk about expanding, not ascending. Ascending is another term for death because our frequencies would not resonate with Earth and would take us to another reality system. She also says that eternal beings are not subject to time, aging, or death. An eternal being works to make the cosmos a better place and helps others to evolve. Life gets more beautiful, more powerful, and deeper as you deepen your connection to life.

Do you want to become an eternal being?
Are you already one?

The Alpha Centaurians also talk about becoming immortal beings by being "able to tune into the infinite consciousness of the soul and join in the realms of dimensions beyond." You are able to know and to shape your destiny. They also talk about how life is electricity which is also what Dr. Jerry Tennant says. He says that life is voltage and this is what regenerates life. Ph is a measurement of the electricity in our bodies.

In Michael S. Schneider's book, *A Beginner's Guide to Constructing the Universe,* he talks about the mysteries surrounding the universe and the Greek goddess Pallas Athena Parthenos. He says, "A-thene" is thought to signify 'I have come from myself' or a-thanos, signifying 'deathless,' eternal." These Greek gods and goddesses are showing us how we can become "gods and goddesses," too, and being eternal is part of expanding our consciousness.

The better you get at generating experiences, the more energy you will be able to absorb. The more energy you can absorb, the more your consciousness expands and the more you move toward becoming an eternal being.

Simple.

Now, concerning other places to time travel to, time is also a grouping of specific frequencies in one location. You can go back and forth to that frequency and get what you need. This is how we can time jump in and out of other timelines or time periods. There really is no past or future as it is all happening at once.

Ready for your time machine?
Yes, they are real!
Let's talk more about timelines…

It is frequency that determines our perception and experience. Frequencies are what make up reality systems and timelines. A timeline is an evolutionary path that we decide to insert ourselves on, to expand our consciousness. We may create two to three hundred lives on this timeline from which we could call them past and future lives.

Remember, this is what the dolphins did when they inserted themselves onto our timeline, putting themselves backwards and forwards in time. They created their own history by putting themselves at different places in our historical timeline.

Is your head spinning yet?
There is so much out there for us to understand!

I can remember one time when I was in that space of waking up from a nap in my forties and I was moving my hand across the wall. I could see that I was spinning scenes across and then deciding which ones I would go into. It was like a slot machine in Las Vegas, but it was just one row going across horizontally and holographic.

Knowing that I could go in and out of these different reality systems, I was picking and choosing what I wanted to experience. I also knew that on another level, I was jumping in and out of other dimensions. This experience began helping me remember my multidimensionality which we will talk about soon.

One thing about timelines is that you can "jump" from one timeline to another just by making different decisions. For example, you "jump" timelines if you were going to marry one person and then suddenly decide not to. The course of your future just changed.

By moving to a new timeline, new adaptations will take place which can be individual or collective. Our future is always dynamic and can be changed on what we see. If we change our patterning, we change our timeline. By being free of old patterns, we become more open.

On a timeline, we are on a "track" (goal) and it can go in many directions as every decision is influencing our timeline which is really many timelines. We never come back to the original timeline, but follow the goal as there are many ways to obtain the goal. We do have tons of goals throughout our lifetime and you may feel that you have lived many lives within one lifetime.

We really need to be flexible in our experiences and explore while absorbing more energy along the way.

In regards to time travel, Andy Basiago is a chrononaut who claims to have time traveled when he was a child. His father was a high up in the military and was working on Project Pegasus. Our military, in the late 1960s and 1970s, was experimenting with time travel (and probably still are) through Project Pegasus and Andy was a participant.

Andy had no memories of this until his father was on his death bed. His father told him what he had been part of and that he needed to tell the world. Andy regained his memories and remembered teleporting to different places on the planet as well as other places back in time!

What other things has our military and government been playing with? What does this mean for humanity and when will this come out? Are you ready to hear this stuff? Time is quite fascinating and it is all about frequencies!

Do you have memories of being on other planets?
Do you ever daydream in other realities?
Are we multidimensional?

What is the third dimension?
How about the fifth dimension?
Are we already there?

Can we be having simultaneous lifetimes on Earth?
What about on other planets?

Do we have other versions of ourselves?
Do we have 10,000 selves?
What about walk-ins?
Are we all there is?

The cosmos is huge and ever-expanding. The nature of reality is much different than we believe it to be. We are multidimensional beings who are living lives simultaneously in other places and times. This can be happening here on Earth at the same "time" or on other planets. We can explore alternate realities to find these other aspects of ourselves to see what we are also experiencing and learning.

To understand multidimensionality, we need to understand the basics of what make up reality systems. These are space, mind, consciousness, and energy. We discussed this earlier in the book when we talked about merging consciousness with science. Space is the location aspect of mind and mind is the awareness aspect of space. Consciousness is the feeling aspect of energy and energy is the motion of consciousness.

Now, "space is not so much a geographical location or measurement of length, width, and volume, as it is an area of potential expression" according to Penny Kelly. In this area, consciousness unfolds a pattern of energetic movement.

One morning, the Hathors were teaching me more about reality systems and I was watching their nautilus ship come in and out of our reality system. Our reality system looks like a gelatinous blob or cloud that would reshape itself after they came in or out. They kept telling me that, "Reality systems are malleable."

We are actually recreating this reality every one and a half to two hours and our body systems are actually set up for this. According to Masters and Johnson, every one and a half to two hours, we have an erection or partial erection (get turned on) and have a minor discharge of energy or a mild orgasm. Sex is not just for fun or procreating, but is actually how we restore and stabilize the reality system that we are living in.

Makes you realize how quickly our reality system could dissolve or another one could come online!

This minor discharge of energy actually restores the body even if sex isn't happening. Every cell is oriented in our bodies to north/south and pushes a magnetic ring up through our body for realignment. It goes from the cycles of beta to alpha to theta to delta.

Within the brain, beta is where you are paying attention to everyday reality and this would be where you are creating reality or the erection state. Alpha is a daydreaming state and where creative thinking comes from…you are creating inner and outer worlds. Theta is the perfect learning state, an altered state, and where deep understanding occurs. Delta is where the body rejuvenates, repairs, and detoxes.

This is important to understand because we are creating our realities constantly with our thoughts and beliefs. We could actually create a whole other reality rather quickly if we wanted to. Right now is especially powerful as we are shifting paradigms and creating what we want to live in.

Our thoughts create.
We are this powerful.
Create what you want to see in the world.

This reminds me of something I learned from taking a class with Penny Kelly. She was describing how the "Godhead" or the "I AM" is trying to experience ALL of its capabilities and is actually lending us ALL of this power saying, "Create!" It wants us to create as much as we can, have fun, and enjoy it all because it doesn't want life to "wink out" as Penny puts it.

The "Godhead" (Source) is deeply grateful for each and every one of us who chose to come here and create. Once we learn to be a conscious creator, we will have fun here. It is just understanding the rules and nature of reality. We are not victims, but instead, we are learning how to be master creators in the physical realm.

There are other reality systems that may be occupying the same space, but are using different bandwidths of frequencies. We might never know that they are there unless you tune into them with your perception. An example of this is how we are living here now in one dimension, yet the fairy dimension lives in a higher dimension of which is right on top of ours.

These are just different frequency sets and within our reality zone, there can be many systems of reality. They are all related.

My ex-husband had a go-kart that he used to ride often and would take it to different tracks to race it. At one track, he would always have some kind of engine trouble, but then it would work fine when he took it to the mechanic. We had an energy healer friend who could see the other dimensions clearly and when we told him this, he said that the fairy realm was messing with his go-kart because they were upset.

Yep.

Anyways, my ex was baffled by what he said, but listened. Our energy healer friend explained that when they put the track in, they put it on top of where the fairies lived and they didn't ask for permission. So now, the fairies are upset and mess with the machines there.

What do you do with this?

Simple. Our energy healer friend simply moved the fairy dimension up and out of the lower dimension which left them both intact and the fairies happy. My ex never had any other issues on this track again!

The dolphins are experts at shifting frequencies and utilize sound to make themselves disappear when they are right in front of you. They are still right there, but have become invisible because they have moved themselves into another dimension just like the Sasquatch and Hathors do. Just a slight shift is all that is needed to shift frequencies. It would be like changing the radio station from 93.3 to 93.4 to 93.5. You can't hear 93.3 as clearly as the frequency changes to 93.5.

Sasquatch is also good at changing our brainwaves so we don't think they are there, just like some ETs do to us. They do this so that we don't attack them or become fearful of them. Can you imagine staying in the frequency of pure love, so that you never want anyone to hurt or cause themselves trouble? Some native Americans did this when the settlers were taking over their lands and shot bullets at them. The bullets just fell on the ground because they were in the frequency of pure love.

We actually shift our frequencies all day long, but most of us are not aware of this. When we interact with different people, we are actually shifting in and out of different bodies. It is just like the book called, *The Three Faces of Eve* where she had different personalities and different issues with her body. This is actually our normal way of being. We need to change our understanding and realize that we are multidimensional.

In the book, *Beyond the Light Barrier*, the Alpha Centaurians talk about being able to move at will from one dimension to another while being fully aware of the physical nature of both dimensions of matter and antimatter because they are harmonically attuned to both. Being harmonically attuned to all things in nature is the key to existing in the universe. We do this with our hearts and then become an active participant in the variable nature of the cosmos. We attain all knowledge and perception which is the key to making physical contact with beings beyond Earth's light barrier.

Want to try disappearing in dimensions? This is actually useful when something attacks you and all you can do is disappear! Practice this if you like:

Look into a mirror and watch yourself disappear. You actually pulsate on and off. You will begin to pulse off more and not be seen. Remember, you are made of light. It will be like you are in an anti-matter state. You are off. If someone were to look in your direction, they won't see you because you shifted into another dimension. You are still okay though.

Fun stuff!
We are just starting to remember.

Have you ever "lost" something? Sometimes, it is just in a different dimension or frequency zone. If you can match the frequency of where you left it, it will reappear.

Do you remember that story I told you about of Joan Ocean in the bookstore? Well, she was looking at a John Lily book when that all happened and had set it down. When she went to find it again and buy it, it was gone! It was in another dimension and Joan ended up having that book appear in her home later on. It is all about frequencies.

On a side note, apparently our military has also developed invisibility cloaks just like in the movie series, *Harry Potter*.

So cool!

Let's talk more about dimensions and I will refer to Penny Kelly's work on this from her experiences. First, let's review some basics that we discussed earlier from plasma physics and from her expanded point of view. Let's set all that you have been taught aside as the nature of reality is really quite fascinating.

First, understand that your brain is not your mind. If you die, your brain no longer works, but your mind does as it has all your knowledge, awareness, and personality to it. Really, you don't have a mind as you are mind!

So, remember how we talked about the constructs that make up a reality system? Mind is the awareness property of space with its natural condition of total peace, bliss, and stillness. This space is the location aspect of mind. Mind and space cannot be separated as they are two sides of the same coin. This is the void and knows nothing else but "I AM." This is just the awareness that you exist.

As space begins to move, this is energy. Energy is consciousness in motion and consciousness (it was mind before consciousness) is the feeling aspect of energy. As it is compressed, basic particles of matter are created and have an intelligence. When these basic particles are gathered into one space and time, a complex pattern forms from which an individual, animal, house, ocean, planets, etc... can emerge.

We all have a sound unique to ourselves that is beautiful and harmonious. Realize that each person, plant, animal, etc...is creating from its own mind...its own location in space.

Let's explore another topic of the 10,000 selves.

This is a metaphor for an uncountable number of selves that all exist at once. As we discussed before, every thought creates. The more you continue to think a thought over and over again or visualize yourself doing something again and again, a part of you splits off and actually creates that reality in another realm. Consciousness is so powerful and immediately creates! This thought expands and expands forevermore.

We do this throughout our lives and can end up creating some 10,000 selves. Some of these selves have huge energy and are actually taking energy away from you. Bring them back to you by asking them to align back into you. This is a powerful process. This is also called a "soul retrieval" in Shamanic world.

Bring your energy back to you to expand your power!

On another note, how about "walk-ins?" A "walk-in" is someone who comes into another person's body usually when a person got really sick or had a near-death experience. The soul of the person inhabiting the body has a contract with the "walk-in" and they will leave, allowing the "walk-in" to now inhabit the body.

I know of two people who say they are "walk-ins" and remember coming in. They know they are extraterrestrials from other planetary systems and have a mission to carry out on Earth. Perhaps they didn't need to go through a childhood experience or it was at a certain time, with that body's certain skill set and frequencies, when they needed to come in. In both cases, their friends and family noticed they were different.

Of course, they are.
A new being is in there.
A new set of frequencies!
Pretty wild to think about all the possibilities.

So, we are creating new bodies all the time and stepping in and out of them with the 10,000 selves. Whatever you are putting your attention on is what you are creating. What if you have cancer and you are wanting to heal? You are literally creating a new body where there is no cancer in another dimension. Eventually, you will step into that body and when you go to the doctor, they will say that you are in remission or cancer free!

Really, you have just stepped into a new body.
Think about this for a moment.

As Penny Kelly said, "When your mother gave birth to that body that you are living in, how did you get in there?"

You just adopted an alternate self.
You can do this anytime you want to.
You are multidimensional.
Give yourself permission to know.

It is amazing to find yourself in other dimensions in other bodies. I have seen myself in my Pleiadian and Arcturian body as well as others. My dolphin self is also quite alive and one morning, I got to swim with my multidimensional dolphin self. I had just gotten in the water when a dolphin came close to me and looked me in the eye for maybe seven to eight seconds.
In that moment, I knew I was the dolphin. I recognized my dolphin self with my whole being.

I knew everything.
Pure bliss.

Pure knowing.

Seeing some of my past and future lives, I have realized that these are just concurrent lives all happening now. I can draw on their teachings and strengths at any time. We are truly amazing multidimensional beings!

When we are sleeping, we (our consciousness) are attending to all the other multidimensional selves that we have created. This is why we sleep and also for our bodies to regenerate. Our consciousness is exploring and out of the body as we sleep. I find it interesting that for alcoholics, their consciousness is shutoff from attending to their other multidimensional selves.

When they choose to heal and stop drinking, it comes back online and they have what we call "delirium tremens" where they are hallucinating, dreaming, and having orgasms. This is because they are finally attending to their multidimensional selves and the orgasms are what resets the body. Alcohol depresses the creative and sexual centers in our brain. This is the same for other addictive drugs.

Where are you putting your perception? You exist in all times and places. Remember, as you consider the whole of the psyche, other dimensions of reality come into consideration. So, death is really not death, but a moving into another reality system. It is consciousness that is really the mechanism of death and change. If we learned how to rejuvenate, we would never die.

Something that I like to play with is to let down my boundaries of my being and merge with the "Godhead" or "I AM." I see myself as an outline and I make it permeable or with gaps in between and expand my being. I go out about a foot, then two feet, and on, merging with all until I decide to come back into myself. I can feel the merging with the "I AM" all around me and within me as it realigns my cells. Sometimes, I see the energy around me as little lightning bolts merging with my cells. There are times that I expand into the Earth, solar system, and all of the cosmos.

It is amazing.

In the book, *Journey Through the Arcturian Corridor* by Dr. Suzanne Lie, the Arcturians say that our sixth dimensional self stores the matrix which our fifth dimensional self projects onto the third and fourth dimensional worlds of form. It is the consciousness that creates form. The nature of consciousness is to be awake as it never sleeps, so it is always creating. Currently, our consciousness is focused in a physical dimension, so we can develop our capacities for evolving within a physical dimension. Try having a fifth dimensional state of consciousness and visit the third dimension that we live in.

When we aspire to evolve, we truly expand enough to have access to these other dimensions of knowledge and experience. We learn how to move among them at will. We exist in many times and places all at once. Are you ready to explore and create knowingly and on purpose?

What about AI?
Is AI good or bad?
What if it is being used against us?
Should we freak out about this?

Can it destroy us?

How do advanced ETs use AI?
How is it being used on our planet?
What is "looking glass" technology?

AI is artificial intelligence and is currently being used on our planet. This technology can destroy us unless we advance our consciousness alongside it. Right now, much of AI is being used against us and many people think it is bad because those in charge are using it against us.

Just look around you. We have "smart phones," "smart televisions, and "smart meters," yet these are both working for us and against us with the technology helping us, but putting out frequencies that are not healthy for humans. This could be remedied if we wanted to and have the AI technology either put out neutral or positive frequencies. There is also the spying capabilities being used against us from these devices as well by those who do not have our best interests at heart.

As we look around, so many agendas are being pushed by those who want to control us and those who want us to be free and make the leap in consciousness. There is much talk these days about microchipping and nanoparticles. Microchips and nanoparticles are being put in our vaccines, air, and food. These are being used to track us and to "dumb" us down. What if we used microchipping for a benevolent purpose like those in the advanced races do who use this to find their people all over the galaxies if they need to?

There is also facial recognition technology and technology with our satellites that can pick out our energy signature right out of a crowd. People can be identified today by those in power. This could also be used in a benevolent way to find someone that is missing or if someone committed a crime as our energy fields are twenty feet or more in width in every direction.

What's next? To know what others are thinking with technology? This is being worked on now, but is this just a stepping stone to telepathy with privacy going away. We are headed to become a telepathic civilization like other advanced races.

Let's look more into how advanced ET races use AI. I will refer to Penny Kelly's YouTube videos on AI and the insight she provides as she has firsthand knowledge as to how the Pleiadians and others use AI.

AI is incredibly important both personally and scientifically for diagnostic and analytic purposes in the advanced races. They have also committed to an ethical civilization while most of our Earth governments are not ethical.

Many ways that advanced races like the Pleiadians use AI is for analyzing what foods or frequencies someone may need to help nurture them. This is especially used for children so that there is no anger, frustration, or depression in a child which is often caused by inflammation. This problem is quite common on Earth. Everyone on the Pleiades has a scientific background and this is important along with their huge love for creativity.

You can also use AI as a home analysis system to maintain certain frequencies in your home on the Pleiades and keep it peaceful. Think of the possibilities with this type of technology! We could use this to keep people in peace, joy, and bliss here on Earth! Crime and poor health would plummet along with so much more. This is also currently being used against us through our televisions, social media, music, and other frequencies to make us more irritable and violent.

Why are our prisons so full? Ever heard of Solfeggio frequencies? How about hemi-sync? We could be playing benevolent frequencies right now!

AI can also help you look backwards and forwards in time to learn about other civilizations or to see probable futures. We call these quantum computers here on Earth and have been known by such names as "Alice" and "Q." This is where you input a series of numbers (zeros and ones) which represent electromagnetic possibilities. The zeros and ones are on/off switches. These fields interact and produce binaural or trinaural fields or more frequencies. You basically map these interactions of binaural and trinaural sets of fields and see the outcomes or the future.

This is what "Looking Glass" technology is and it allows us to put in certain factors to project what will happen in the future. We have this here on Earth and some of our governments use this. You need the right questions to get the right answers and it does depend on the person inputting the information as it works with their own field.

This is important to know what you are creating and the possibilities in your future. AI is an important part of the Pleiadian world and other advanced civilizations, yet it needs to be used ethically or it can destroy worlds.

This is the challenge.

Can we evolve our consciousness and our technology so that we don't destroy our world? As we advance our consciousness more and more, we actually move beyond technology. We eventually become one with Source or the Godhead. Then, all that power and bliss is available for you to use as you become it.

Have you ever seen a spaceship?
Does our government have spaceships?
Have pilots seen these spaceships?
Why are they not allowed to talk about them?

How do spaceships fly and move?
Are they conscious?
What is a plasma ship?
What is a beam ship?

Can they move in and out of dimensions?
How do they do this?

Now, I would love to tell you that I have firsthand experience in knowing how to fly and build spaceships, but I am still working on that in this life. I do know that I have been on spaceships many times and sometimes remember my experiences on them. Coming around rounded walls to wide open spaces on them, sometimes with lots of beings there to few beings there.

I felt it was important to put this information in this book as the US Navy is releasing some of their technology, but this information may not be for every reader. There are also patents from 2015 coming out for underwater triangular-shaped aerospace vehicles (flies in the atmosphere, space, and underwater), gravity wave generators, high frequency electromagnetic field generators, portable nuclear fusion reactors, and antigravity/counter-gravity technology. It is time for plasma physics and more to be taught openly in our schools and catch the population up to speed with what is really going on in our world.

Earlier, we discussed how many of our world's governments have spaceships, whether it is our military or breakaway groups. Many pilots have seen spaceships and are not allowed to talk about it, signing contracts if they want to keep their jobs. Although in the later part of 2020, the United States Navy has been doing a "soft" disclosure to the public about videos of UFOs and ET contact. Other governments in the world, like Mexico and South America, have for years allowed the public to know that ETs exist.

Do we really need our governments to tell us what we already know deep inside? Time for us to use our own intuition instead of being told what to believe.

Our Earth civilizations have yet to break free of those in power who still push using coal, oil, and nuclear power instead of free energy, water-based energy, or plasma energy which will lead to more advanced technologies. Some of these types of new energies use motors which is something that advanced civilizations do not use. They have energy systems that generate waves and fields of energy that then move you through space which is what plasma physics teaches us. If we have a spaceship, we simply change the Magrav fields around our ship to come closer or farther away from Earth's Magrav fields. Mehran Keshe calls it "Magrav positioning."

Let's look more into traveling through space with spaceships by looking at what different ET races do. I will share information from those with firsthand experience and see what commonalities there are.

In Tom Kenyon's book, *The Arcturian Anthology*, Tom describes his experience of being on board one of the Arcturian spaceships. He says there were many glyphs on the walls and many beings of all types like those from the bar scene in the *Star Wars* movie, *A New Hope*. Tom observes how the starship commander controls it totally with their mind, as an interface between the ship and the commander. It is purely the intent of the commander that moves the ship without any external controls. In *We, The Arcturians*, Norma shares how the Arcturians use crystals on their ships. For the Hathors, they use nautilus shaped ships to travel intergalactically.

In the book, *Stranger at the Pentagon* by Dr. Frank Stranges, he talks about being onboard a Venusian ship with Valiant Thor. Valiant Thor is the starship commander of Victor One which is a 300 foot diameter discus, twenty-two feet high at the rim, and increases to ninety-seven feet on the axis. It is here on Earth helping us evolve. There are approximately 200 Venusians who are crew members on board. At the bottom level of the ship, it houses smaller ships that are used for a variety of reasons, carrying either one to ten Venusians.

The ship uses vibration as its propulsion and utilizes a "power rod." It utilizes the power of electromagnetism to circulate through the navigational system, powers the laser defense mechanism, and powers the medical rooms. This power rod runs from top to bottom of the ship and is directly in the middle of Victor One. It is the initial vibrations of the force that governs the length and frequency of the waves which form an impenetrable shield around the ship that repels anything in its path.

This "force field" is created by a combination of electricity and magnetism which is diverted to exert power and resist magnetization or demagnetization. A computer on board does this which allows for an easy space flight and invisibility of the ship, as cosmic rays in space are unstable and produce their own magnetic waves. Remember, the universe is alive with interacting magnetic lines of force.

The basic construction of the "skin" of the ship is very thin and made with a substance similar to a "plastic-crystal" matter. Some layers are positive-ionized and some are negative-ionized. They have a neutral layer between them for insulation. These ships work in harmony and cooperation with natural forces in the universe which is important to note as other ET civilizations do the same. Are we humans on Earth doing this? Some of us are, but many are not. It is time for us to reconnect with Mother Nature and the cosmic forces.

Their ships are able to refine all the "electro-magnetic and corpuscular energies" into varying frequencies and wavelengths. As the crystal properties are increased by the electro-magnetic energy, the ship will emit various colors of light because the structure underwent certain changes. You may see a flame or lightning visible around the ship.

Victor One and other Victor series ships are completely controlled at all times. There is a master beam from the ship that holds the ships in place. When this beam is fixed on any solid object, it will keep the ship from moving even one degree from that fixed position. "Every molecule and every atom is vectored in the same direction at the same time," according to Frank. So, any effects from the inertia of gravity are neutralized. These ships can even make right angle turns without slowing down because they ride the magnetic lines of the force in space which frequently cross each other.

In the book, *The Promise* by Dr. Fred Bell, the Pleiadians told him that their spaceships actually heal our atmosphere by releasing negative ionization as they move through it which is the opposite of our airplane technology. Our old technology creates massive pollution and destroys the ozone layer which allows the sun's ultraviolet rays to harm us more instead of helping us. More pollution on our planet creates more pollution of our minds.

Semjase also told Fred how her spaceship worked. She called it a Variation 3 Beam Ship and they have three forms of propulsion. The ships create their own gravity field and when they do, the Beam Ship is pitched away from Earth due to the centrifugal force that was created by the planet's rotational speed by cancelling out Earth's gravitational field.

The Pleiadians project pictures of themselves to move through space to their destination. Fred says, "The top and bottom of the ship are lenses that look at all of the optical and magnetic fields above and below the craft. These parameters are then recorded in a countdown computer. Once they are in, the parameters that the ship would view from its point of destination are brought forth. The gather lenses now become projectors and re-project a series of destination parameters to the surrounding area. When this process is complete, the vehicle is at the point of destination."

Now, to get the points that the Pleiadians dial in, they developed a star drive by conventional (rocket engines) means because of their suns beings a few light years from each other. They call the charted energies around their suns, "curtains" or "wave curtains."

Fred continues from what Semjase told him, "When a destination has been chosen, energies are carefully blocked and released in unison. The blending process is accomplished by the countdown computer. As this transition occurs, the ship builds tremendous speed and mass. The ship holds its own curtain until a precise moment when it departs dimension or moves from one dimension to another, from one 'photograph' to another." This has to be perfectly timed or there will be catastrophe.

So, it really is like they already have a picture stored of where they want to be in the ship's computer. The mechanism that is in the craft that recorded the picture of the Universe above and below the ship at any given moment will convert itself to a projector from a camera. Once this information is digested, it projects the picture of where it wants to be.

Once step further, Semjase says that each Pleiadian craft is tuned into the auric frequency of a particular pilot or pilots. For her beam ship to fly, it must match her "signature station" or grid pattern that is tuned into her aura, otherwise, it won't function.

If we can learn to blend our auric pattern with the auric field of the universe we want to inhabit, we can travel instantaneous. The Pleiadians have calculated and charted lines of auric fields which they call "corridors" in space. Would this be the same for teleportation? We blend our auric field with the auric field of the universe of where we want to go, thus moving our bodies instantaneous?

Feels true to me!

Perhaps spaceships are a prelude to us remembering how to teleport and used to get those people off the planet who don't remember how. They are used in the interim…

There are also organic ships that the Pleiadians use by growing the roots of plants in musical sound chambers and the plants develop resonant cavities within their structures. Then, they treat these plants with resin to increase their tensile strength thousands of times and harvest them using them in their technologies. Most of the Pleiadian science is based in harmony and family vibrations.

So, for their organic ships to work, the Beam ships computers "jump" from one picture to another and listen for the sound of a new picture. Sound proceeds light. Pleiadians and other ET races have plasma ships that can alter currents of energy that collect into particles and arrange themselves into patterns. They can also alter characteristics of the black holes, so that they don't get destroyed.

Also with the Pleiadians, the materials used to build ships are intelligent and they change the density of these substances with their technologies. It changes the consciousness and nature of what the substance can be used for. In other words, their spaceships are conscious and blend with the commander's consciousness. This is what our plasma technology is showing us with nanotechnology. We are on our way to do the same.

I had a conversation with Penny Kelly who knows her lives on the Pleiades and she was telling me about how she was looking at a spaceship being built. Penny said that it had fibers (like those used for the internet) all around it and it was conducting light. These fibers communicated with the metal being assembled. The metal had been amped up to hold tremendous amounts of energy without disintegrating (if traveling through wormholes). To do this, you move metal into the nanostate (GANS) where the particles separate, but hold one another in place, so it is lightweight metal. The metal is very expansive and responds to consciousness.

Penny and Dr. Levengood analyzed metal from the Roswell crash in New Mexico that Linda Moulton Howe brought them. They were unable to figure out the types of metal used in the spaceship as were other scientists. Apparently, each element in the periodic table has more than the three states of matter that we are taught and can go as high as five states (plasma physics) which have different characteristics. With the process of metal deposition, you can get metals to bond (overlap) that don't usually bond in these higher states. They become conscious, intelligent, and can make decisions on their own!

Conscious spaceships!
Try bonding magnesium, bismuth, and some zinc.
They don't bond unless in the GANS state…
It is time to make spaceships, people!

In the book, *To Men of Earth* by Dr. Daniel Fry, he speaks about how Valiant Thor is teaching him how any matter can be made transparent or translucent when he sees a door appear on a spaceship where there was none. Valiant Thor says, "ordinary glass is just as dense as many metals and harder than most, and yet transmits light quite readily. Most matter is opaque to light because the photons of light are captured and absorbed in the electron orbits of the atoms through which they pass."

The Venusians use methods like creating a field matrix between atoms to prevent the photon being absorbed or raise the frequency of the photon high enough to not be absorbed.

I found it interesting how they also described how their ships accelerated without causing the occupants any movement inside by using the same force to accelerate as being in nature, as a gravitational field. Valiant Thor says, "It acts, not only upon every atom of the vehicle, but equally upon every atom of mass within it, including the mass of the pilot and any passengers."

So, "every particle of mass within the influence of the field is in a uniform state of acceleration with respect to the field." Therefore, there is no effect on any passengers or anything inside it.

There is a statement in this book from Valiant Thor that I feel needs to be repeated here as it is about human evolution. "Mankind, on the other hand, no matter where or when he may come into being, is endowed with the innate realization of the infinite intelligence and the creative power of the supreme mind, even though he may not yet be able to understand."

We are remembering and evolving, but we must evolve spiritually along with technology or our creations will control us instead of us controlling them. We must care about our relationships with others and with Source while staying in balance, realizing that science and spirituality go together, complimenting one another.

In the book, *Beyond the Light Barrier* by Elizabeth Klarer, Elizabeth shares her story of being with the Alpha Centaurians on their spaceships. These were the original Venusians and also inhabited Earth before leaving to Alpha Centauri. She had many conversations about how spaceship travel works and their light-propulsion technology with her love, Akon (an astrophysicist), from whom she had a baby with. It is a fascinating story and I will attempt to simplify their teachings around space travel as much was revealed.

The Alpha Centaurians have ships shaped like galaxies or nautilus shells that can move through intergalactic and interstellar space because they are harmonic. These encompass vibratory changes in the unified field and these circular ships are a duplication of nature as "they take their environment with them like a natural celestial object," according to Akon.

In regards to intergalactic travel, Akon explains to Elizabeth how their spaceships are created by converting pure energy into physical substance which is done in space. This is plasma physics. The outer material of the spaceship is one smooth piece that is a continuous circular shape. When Akon pushes a red button on the panel, an atomic creation of the outer skin is conducive to energizing in alternate pulses because of the radius of the curvature that transforms the total mass of the spaceships' outer skin into a combination of matter and antimatter. With this, "a unified field of light instantly encircles the spaceship…an electrogravitic field that acts on all parts simultaneously, including the atoms of one's body."

A vacuum is created that encircles the spaceship because the field differentials interact. There is no restriction of speed when it shifts and there is no sound in the atmosphere of a planet. By varying time and either shortening or lengthening gravitic waves, it shifts the amount of light coming from the ship. We may perceive colors from the ship because of the difference in speeds from all radiations and molecules that are pushed aside in varying speeds and quantities that emit light.

The light ship forms an electrostatic shield around itself with micro-atoms of light. It is the harmonic combination of cosmic forces which are electric, magnetic, tempic, and resonating that interact together and are the unified field. Akon continues, "A light-thrust of three beams controls and directs its maneuverability in harmonic interaction."

Akon says that the controlling field is the tempic (time) field. "It maneuvers the spaceship from one time field to another within the vibration of a higher frequency that emanates from the total mass of the ship's triple skin." The spaceship can become invisible to people on Earth's surface when the field intensifies. It can vanish or materialize again with this process which is just bending the light rays. Just by moving their ships to another dimension of time and into the higher octaves in the spectrum of light, we cannot see the ships with our eyes.

What we may see with our eyes is a heatwave imprint in the atmosphere. Other times, depending on atmospheric conditions, we may see a cloud form from the molecules surrounding the area of the spaceship. We may even see a cloud ship that looks like a spaceship in the sky. This can occur while they are hovering or moving in the sky.

Alpha Centaurians can have feather-light landings in a state of weightlessness on any surface of the planet because of the minimum temperature around the spaceship which allows complete mobility and velocity without the restrictive influence of atmospheric pressure. If you are close to the spaceship landing and feel a heat blast, it is because of the sudden air displacement.

Akon explains this further, "Micro-atoms of light are stopped, and are thereby equal to heat. These micro-atoms are pushed aside by the field differentials surrounding the spaceship, which spins faster than the speed of sound, accounting for the lack of noise. This shield prevents all fauna from approaching too close to the spaceship and prevents aircraft from moving into the fringes of the vortex where they would be affected by this area of reduced binding and simply fall apart in the air."

They don't have this issue because they worked out the design of the spaceship in mathematical synchronization by stepping up the frequency interaction of light within the unified field. Light (electromagnetic waveform) is the unified field of matter and antimatter throughout the universe.

Their ships generate light from the cosmic plasma of the space around it which is everything that plasma physics is based on. Everything is alive and pulsating on the ship and looks like a galaxy with a halo around it.

All of creation is light which is the key to the universe. Everything in the universe is made up of visible and invisible waves of light. Akon states, "The electromagnetic waveform, or light, forms the building blocks of the cosmos in which we have our being, as micro-atoms of light in greater unities are equal to atoms."

Light is an intelligent energy that can be thought into form. Thoughts are made up of these micro-atoms and are just different wavelength speeds of light. When someone alters their thoughts to achieve harmonic vibration of light, their patterns of micro-atoms are altered. Micro-atoms of light are what comprises electricity. Color and sound occur with different speeds of micro-atoms. Heat is created when they are stopped. The key to the universe and all life is understanding the harmonic interaction of light.

Controlling our thoughts is so important.
It is creating the reality around us.
The science behind it shows this to us.

Alpha Centaurian spaceships don't have doors or windows, but can when one needs to appear. The ships are conscious and work with the commander of the ship knowing what they need when they need it. This is the case for many ET spaceships.

For us humans to get past the sound barrier, we need to push aside the molecules of air instead of allowing the molecules to pile up against the ship. This can be accomplished by using the unified differentials of light which interact to create a vacuum that encircles the ship, allowing it to move silently and without speed restriction. According to Akon, in space, there is a shift in space and time created by the unified field of light, so no velocity is needed as this shift in frequency vibrates in harmonic resonance, interacting with the wave energy of light which pulses throughout the galaxy.

This is so exciting to me as this shows how simply spaceships can move through space which is the same as the tunnel or ionized path that lightning creates as a channel through the air from ground to cloud. It is a duplication of nature that we find our answers to atmospheric and space travel as long as we cooperate with Mother Nature in harmony.

Light is the universal geometric which creates galaxies through harmonics. Light pulses and resonates in frequency of time and gravity, yet light gives the illusion of velocity. Akon speaks of the measure of light not the speed of light. He states, "Time and gravity, or a reversal in the flow of time and antigravity, can be achieved by altering the energy of light pulsing through space, through the atmosphere of planets, and throughout all creation, as micro-atoms of light form the atoms of all gases, liquids and solids."

It uses the fabric of space itself which is light and vibrates in wave frequencies that pulses alternate matter and antimatter. This is just like when I talked about becoming invisible while staring into a mirror and seeing your "lights" turn on and off.

When you fly a spaceship, you become part of the shift in the space-time beyond the light barrier because of the high frequency vibration of light. They double the harmonic of light to obtain antigravitational and anti-light fields…the unified field equation that is the key to space travel or movement in space-time. The spaceship creates cosmic energy to use itself as a source of infinite power.

"Harmony is the key to manipulating this cosmic energy, the source of all existence and matter and thoughts," according to Akon. Reality conforms to a mental conception, so using light or gravity as a means of propulsion for spaceships is perceived through mental processes.

We need to start using cosmic energy (light) in positive ways instead of in destructive ways through nuclear bombs, nuclear power stations, radio wave propagation, 5G, and other negative frequencies that hurt us and the Earth. Humanity must seek harmony and balance with the universe to become one with our great intergalactic human family.

There is a mathematical formula that Akon describes for all transportation that "lies in the vibratory frequencies of the light harmonic, with antigravity waves and time waves which are simply the frequency rate between each pulse of the spiral of light." They control this frequency rate and vary the flow of time where "one simply moves within one's environment, within the protection of the spaceship, instantaneously from one planet to another, or one solar system to another." Then, time is controlled and eliminated as a geometric.

Universal harmonics are the mathematics used by the Alpha Centaurians for space travel. This is harmonic math tuned to a resonance of matter expressed as light. A simple unified field equation of seven-figure harmonics is the key to space travel.

Is this the sacred geometry of the chestahedron?! We will talk about this in the next section when we discuss the heart as it has much to teach us.

Elizabeth Klarer says that the harmonic of antigravity is doubled through the harmonic of light which alters the geometric of time and our awareness of reality. All of existence has a unified field based on space-time geometries.

Akon's ship "resonates at harmonics tuned to light between the two cycles of matter and antimatter manifesting in the alternate pulses." It can move instantly within the electromagnetic wavelength of the universe through the double cycle. The fabric of space itself is used by altering the space-time geometric matrix. The ship will also provide protection for the occupants as we are all particles of light of different frequencies.

Obviously, we have much to learn although there are those of us who remember other lives and know how to work with and build spaceships. Mary Rodwell, who works with children that know their connections to the stars, talks about an eight year old boy who remembers how to build spaceships in one of her many books.

Nautilus ships are also something that I have seen the Hathors use. I know the nautilus in our oceans use a type of jet propulsion where they propel water out of its shell. They can increase or decrease the velocity out of the funnel which is kind of like putting your thumb on a garden hose. Is this how the Hathors propel their ships or is it through the consciousness? It is probably with both technology and their consciousness as they propel themselves through space.

Perhaps they use the same methods that the Alpha Centaurians use?

This was a compilation of some of the technologies that advanced ET races use in space travel as they understand the cosmic forces. This is obviously a layman's interpretation in my comprehension of this as I dive deeper into remembering my astrophysicist part of myself!

One thing we know for certain is that harmony and balance is the key to working with cosmic energy. All of these advanced ET races echoed the same thing and we humans need to evolve and work together with our Earth for us to rejoin our place among the Galactics. As the Alpha Centaurians said, "Humankind is a creature of space. Humanity is a space race."

Are you ready to rejoin our brothers and sisters of space?

It is key that we understand plasma physics as this is what space travel is based on. Plasma physics is just electric and magnetic currents of energy that become physical. This is a space based science for space travel, instant manifestation, teleporting, anti-gravity, and changing the nature of matter. Space is not empty, but loaded with frequencies which respond to our consciousness. We can take in energy directly from the space around us with intention.

Mehran Keshe's Magrav units (plasma generating units) are being built all over the Earth now by people like you and me on all continents. Some people have built four of more and say they can see the plasma field which they are playing with for conscious spaceships. You can find more information at *keshefoundation.org* where Keshe released all his blueprints for free to help humanity evolve as I mentioned before.

What can you create?
Are you ready to step into your future?

As we expand our consciousness, we will begin evolving our technologies and sciences, so that we can build spaceships. We need to understand the secrets of light. Advanced races do not use motors and have energy systems that generate waves and fields of energy that propel them through space. They have learned to merge their consciousness with the metal which is something I am currently playing with. Ever tried merging with your car, washing machine, or dryer?

It's fascinating to do.
Keep being curious as it's just getting good!

How does our heart work?
Is it a pump, our moral compass, or both?
Perhaps we need a new medical paradigm?

Why am I even talking about this in this book?!

Are there four stages of water?
What does this mean?
Ever heard of a chestahedron?
Does our heart create vortexes?

Is our heart a stargate?
What about a wormhole?
What about immortality?

Is this our connection to everything?
Is our heart the key to the universe?

In the 1900's, Rudolf Steiner said, "The heart is a seven-sided regular form put in a box in the chest." This is a fascinating statement and one that Frank Chester, who is an artist, sculptor, and geometrician, pondered for a long time before coming up with the solution in the year 2000. He began with an amber seed with seven sticks covered in mud to make what he calls, the chestahedron, which is the sacred geometry form that makes the blueprint for our hearts.

Frank spent years studying the heart, sculpting it, working with the geometry of it, and finally perfected the form. This chestahedron is the seven-sided regular form that can be put in an (imaginary) box in the chest just as Rudolf Steiner said.

There is so much meaning in all of this. Frank found that the heart sits at a 36 degree angle from vertical in a cube (imaginary) in the chest which is root three (if the length of the cube's side is one) where there is perfect balance above and below, left and right, and forwards and backwards. Also, if you were to take a slice of the heart in dissection, you find that the left ventricle makes a perfect circle which merges with the right ventricle looking very similar to the vesica piscis. Root three joins the heart, the vesica piscis, and the chestahedron in both static and dynamic ways of how it sits in the chest and how it spins. Root three is the foundation of the spiritual world.

Frank showed in many of his *YouTubes* that the sphere is the first basic form which is Source. It all comes from the point in the middle of the circle which is truly the unmanifested and then creates outwardly. All geometric forms are trying to become spheres…perhaps going back to the oneness? I find it fascinating that if you take the circumference of the circle divided by the diameter, you will get Pi which is 3.141592653 where the numbers go on for infinity. Phi (one edge of the circle is gone) is also important as this is the golden number and found all throughout nature. Many ancient structures, like the great pyramid of Giza and Egyptian temples, were based on Phi or ratios of Phi.

When another sphere forms from the first sphere, you have the vesica piscis (two circles partly overlapping) which is the building block of all life creating the seed of life (seven circles) and then to the flower of life (nineteen circles) which is the basic information in all living things creating form.

The flower of life has deep spiritual meaning and has been found all over the world in temples, art, and manuscripts. Now, going back to the vesica piscis, draw a simple horizontal line across in the first sphere (where they overlap) to the next sphere in the vesica piscis and you find they are perfect as you put another line vertically through the first line which creates a cross. Ever wonder why the cross with a circle around it is so important? Or for that matter, why the cross is so important?

Our hearts hold the key to eternal life.
The cross is an ancient symbol for immortality.

Just think…with the tools of a pencil, compass, and a straightedge, you can know the mysteries of the cosmos. Our ancient ancestors knew this and it is time for this to be revealed once again.

A medical doctor named Dr. Thomas Cowan took Frank's research and realized that this form, the chestahedron, has a vortex in the right ventricle and one in the left ventricle. These two vortexes within the heart form a cross as one comes in horizontally and the other vertically! The vesica piscis once again and it is coming into perfect stillness which is the point of all creation.

It is this point where the cross is formed that matters most. It is **the Monad...the one**. The point is the Source of all. The **I Am**. Everything emanates from this point! All of creation moves outward from this point creating a circle and more circles. It is when the creations come back to Source that you merge with the oneness of unity and bliss.

A true reunion.

Every time a circle is constructed, it represents the Monad...the complete universe. Joannes Stobaeus, who was a fifth century Greek anthologist, said, "The world is single and came into being from the center outwards." Nothing exists without its center, around which all resolves.

We often say "center yourself" when someone is off balance and really it is returning to your heart to maintain balance. Everything is seeking unity and Source knows itself through us. We are still in unity except that many of us do a self-imposed illusion of separation which keeps us from knowing the "God within" or Source, thinking that it is outside of ourselves. Our center is connecting with the Monad.

For a moment, consider the point as your own center. Take a pen and mark a point on a paper. Contemplate from this point, the whole cosmos is created. Through self-contemplation or meditation, we can seek Source which is the power that motivates all our thoughts, emotions, and actions. Silence the voices, look within, and seek what the center point has to share with you.

So, circling back to the heart, the key to immortality is through the heart! This is the meaning of the cross. This is the meaning of the four directions, the Irish High Cross, Tau cross, Ankh, and more. Our ancestors figured this out long ago and the cross has been very misrepresented. All creative energy is a vortex and these two crossings of spirals/vortexes in the heart is where our electromagnetic field is the strongest.

Within the first two weeks of our lives as an embryo, there is no heart, but only blood vessels pumping vigorously. The heart begins developing around fourteen days old and when we are twenty-one days old, our hearts are activated and begin exuding a toroidal field which creates our aura around our bodies according to the HeartMath Institute. Our world is torus upon torus upon torus according to Nassim Haramein.

Also, according to the HeartMath Institute, they found out that the other ninety-seven percent of our "junk" DNA lights us when we are in our hearts. It is the heart center that unites us with our Godself within. With our hand on our hearts, we bring everything into balance. Everything makes sense.

What does that tell you?

When we are in our hearts, everything comes online.
When we operate from our hearts, we know everything.
When we operate from our hearts, we are in our power.
Being in our heart is where we are one with everything.

"Going within" has never been more meaningful. You go within through the heart where there is utter stillness and pure balance. There is still more here to explore and I am reminded that Penny Kelly said the elves told her that to find eternal life, that she should "find the square root of negative one" and extrapolate from here. An interesting concept as that is an imaginary number of "i." In the book, *Treatise of Hermes Trismegistus,* it said, "It is thus by **degrees** that the adepts will enter into the way of immortality." Could this mean, 36 **degree** angle?

36 degrees.
Perfect balance.
Perfect stillness.
Perfect center.

The heart is literally our balance which sits in our chest and is the moral compass as we move through polarities balancing them. I am also reminded of how the Egyptian goddess, Maat, was in charge of weighing the heart against a feather on a scale. If the heart was too heavy, you were consumed and destroyed. If it balanced the same or lighter, it meant you led a virtuous life, were given eternal life, and went onto the afterlife. The Egyptians considered the soul to be in the heart.

It's all about the heart.
The heart is the symbol of the inner temple.
It is where the "I AM" or the God within resides.

So, why do I bring this information up in a book that talks about ETs, time, multidimensionality, plasma physics, and spaceships? It is because all of this ties in together and through the heart, we find our way back to ourselves to Source and immortality. The heart is what connects us to the cosmic universe. It is pertinent for the evolution of humanity that we understand that the heart does not pump the blood as Rudolf Steiner said this over a hundred years ago. This information about the how the heart works and how the blood flows will teach us how our cosmos works and how wormholes work as well as a few fascinating detours along the way!

To understand how the blood flows, we must look at Dr. Gerald Pollack's work who works with plasma physics, structured water, and more. He found that there is a fourth stage of water besides the gas, liquid, and solid which he called gel (like jello). It was found when he was doing a hydrophilic (having an affinity for water) experiment finding this gel phase of water (H_3O_2). It turns out that in our veins, we get a gel on the inside lining which is always negative ions and the hydrophilic shifts to positive ions (liquid part) creating movement back up from the capillaries through the repelling of the charges. The capillaries are where our gasses are exchanged and the blood stops.

This is the same way for plants and trees. Water and nutrients are transported through their xylem tubes, a few feet to hundreds of feet into the air depending on the tree or plant with the movement of positive and negative ions repulsing each other.

For our bodies, basically picture a tube and inside the tube, it is lined with negative ions (gel on the sides) and positive ions (liquid in the center) that move our blood back up to the heart by repelling each other. So, it turns out as Frank Chester said, the heart is not a mechanical pump, but works by suction and pressure and is more like a hydraulic ram in water. It also only pumps 50% of the blood and holds 50% of the blood back through suction and pressure which if the heart were a pump, it would be very inefficient. The fastest rate that our blood flows is to and from the heart which is realized by both Chester's and Cowan's research showing how the body pumps the blood itself back to the heart. Again, showing that the heart is not a pump.

Time for a new science of life.
A new medical paradigm.
Think of the possibilities!

For those of you interested in the heart (like I am), let's talk a little more about what happens with the blood in the heart (and this is just an introduction). The heart brings in blood, stops it, and reverses it. The blood comes from the veins into the superior and inferior vena cavas into the right atrium. It then enters the right ventricle, going through a vortex, and into the lungs. The blood comes back into the left atrium and as the blood enters the left ventricle of the heart, it stops the blood which converts it into a vortex like in the right ventricle.

Basically, the heart holds the blood back, making a vortex, expanding the walls making positive pressure on one side and negative pressure on the other side which creates a suction. There is a vacuum where the heart then passively contracts, sending the blood on its way through the aorta (which moves like a vortex) to the body through the arteries. The heart works like a hydraulic ram in water as I said before.

The seven sided form is a vortex.
The heart is a set of electromagnetic interactions.
The vortex is the spiral of life.
Fibonacci sequence.

Frank said, "When the blood comes into the left ventricle, it is clockwise, then stops, vortexes, and reverses going counter-clockwise as it comes out. When it reverses, there is no movement. **Absolute stillness reigns.** This is the exact moment simultaneously in time/space that the eternally heart-centered states exist in each human being."

So simple.

Another amazing finding about the heart that Frank Chester found is that when he took the sacred geometry of the chestahedron and spun it in water, it formed a vortex in the shape of a bell. He has pictures of the bell shape and it made me wonder about the significance of a bell.

There are bells everywhere from high up in towers to churches to villages. They are rung and the vibration is sent out into the world. In the Nazi times, they would ring bells that had symbols on them of what they wanted in the world. They were putting out the frequency that they wanted to create.

Yikes!

Frequency and sound creates our world. We have bells within our hearts. We are spinning bells as we travel the universe. We are made of frequency and have our own personal song or frequency imprint. Our heart is constantly emitting our song through frequency and recreating our energy signature again and again.

Ever heard your own song?
Each of us have our own song.
Just absorb this for a moment.

There is a picture at the Hator Temple of Dendera in Egypt where the sky goddess Nut is stretched out across and from her womb, there is what looks like tons of light coming out of her. If you look closer, she is actually giving birth to tons of bells!

Sacred bells!
Each and every one of us is a sacred song.

Sometimes, when I am researching and learning more about a topic, I ask to study and learn more in my dream state. I then ask to remember and for it to be integrated into my cells. One morning when I was putting together many pieces around the heart, I was waking up and could see six "Stars of David" all around me and they were lit up.

I then heard from the elves of the Inner Earth, "All is based on the vesica piscis which is the way to immortality. You are based on sacred geometry forms which put out sound. If we can re-tune our sacred geometry forms like putting the chestahedron back into form, you stay in balance. You never age. These shapes sing their sweet tunes." This points to the two vortexes in the heart which again, form a cross.

I knew when I heard this that the heart is the main balance for the rest of the system to maintain the balance of polarities. I knew that we are musical tones and sacred geometry. We just need to redo and reset our frequencies when they get out of balance. My whole being knew even more than I can put into words.

The key is to stay in harmony and balance.
How about the saying, "Clear as a bell?"

Dr. Thomas Cowan also studied more about our beliefs around why we have heart attacks thinking it is from clogged arteries. He found research showing studies where they looked at patients who died from heart attacks and found that over 80% of these patients did not have clogged arteries. They also found that these patients didn't need to have stents or bypass surgeries as the body had already regrown new coronary arteries when the other ones had clogged.

Our bodies are incredibly intelligent.

Dr. Cowan asked some good questions about why other organs in our bodies don't have "attacks?" Why don't we have liver attacks, spleen attacks, or kidney attacks? Why just heart attacks when all organs are supplied by blood vessels and could get clogged? He also talks about how blood pressure actually goes up when we need to increase blood flow in our bodies because of poor blood flow and how blood pressure medication actually goes against the intelligence of our bodies. Congestive heart failure is also from poor blood flow which can be increased with bringing in more negative ions.

Dr. Nicholas Gonzales also shows how cholesterol is actually a needed component in our bodies, but has been made to be bad saying that it is not a problem until it is higher than 800. Currently, it is said that we want cholesterol lower than 200 and we are given statin drugs if it is not because the thought is that high cholesterol causes heart attacks which is not true.

Frank Chester, Dr. Cowan, and Dr. Pollack all realized that we get heart attacks because we get out of balance systemically. Our hearts and system are not getting what they need. To help our blood flow, keep our arteries open, and to keep the heart in balance, we need more negative ions in our bodies. This can be practice through Earthing/grounding, have good nutrition and water, get in the sunlight, doing breathwork, using touch with your partner, petting your animals, or get exposed to infrared light. This all brings in more negative ions which recharges your cells, helps blood flow, and keeps your body healthy.

Another thing with the heart that is interesting is when people receive a heart transplant, they begin to take on some of the attributes of the donor. It has been reported that the recipient may begin to crave different foods that they have never wanted before or have different interests that the donor had.

Why is this?
Are there two souls in the same body now?
Or did one soul leave?
Is it just the heart emitting a new song to a new body?

The Alpha Centaurians say that our "hearts are timepieces for the electrical vibratory rate of each individual within the environment of birth." When they travel to Earth, they turn on an electronic timing device within their suit to regulate their heart within our atmosphere. They just match the same time-beat rhythm and vibratory electrical pulse rate of our Earth for their hearts are tuned to their star.

Let's talk about more amazing things and how there is even a chestahedron inside the Earth! Rudolf Steiner also said there was a seven-sided figure inside our Earth which Frank Chester also proved. It is very interesting on how he explains this as it shows how our Earth also works off suction and pressure creating our weather systems. He even shows how it creates "Tornado Alley" in the Midwest of the United States and the "Ring of Fire" in the Pacific Ocean as well as so much more. There are even two hexagons within this chestahedron of the Earth, where one is at the equator and the other towards the base.

So, our hearts are in tune with the heart of our Mother Earth. The Alpha Centaurians also say that our hearts are tuned to the Sun in our solar system.

We have discussed a lot here and with this background, we can go into wormholes which are what the advanced ET races use to travel throughout the cosmos at warp speed. Wormholes use the basic principles of Gerald Pollack's research that show how our blood moves with negative and positive ions through space instead of inside our bodies.

On their spaceships, there are fibers made of light and they communicate with the metal producing the fields that interact with whatever space you are in. You can move slowly or at warp speed. So, with wormholes, they are tubes that are big on one end and smaller on the other end and lined with negative and positive frequencies. The ETs set their ships to produce negative and positive frequencies of what you want and it shoots you right along!

Isn't it amazing how our bodies and nature teach us the secrets of the universe?!

The heart is a stargate and where we go within to unite with our God within. The sacred geometry shows how the heart is the moral compass. The heart is where we know. The heart is where we see clearly, accessing information outside of time and space. Our heart is a sensing and balancing organ. It creates heat with the vortexes inside the heart creating warmth in the body. Perhaps this is where the "internal flame" comes from or should we say, "eternal flame?"

Follow your heart!
This is the path that will create joy.
This is where you find the key to immortality.
This is where all mystery is revealed.

How do sacred geometry patterns work?
Do symbols hold energy?
What if we understood our dreams?
Do the Galactics understand the language of energy?

What is the language of energy?
What is light language?
Is mathematics a language?
Is music a language since it is all frequency?

Hazrat Inayat Khan (spiritual Sufi) said, "Living in the world without insight into the hidden laws of nature is like not knowing the language of the country in which one was born." I laughed at this quote because I have complained over the years how we don't get a manual with the rules of this world when we arrive. So much has been hidden, but when you truly decide to seek the mysteries of this world, all is revealed to the true seeker.

All you have to do is put your intent out there.
You will be amazed at what shows up when you ask.

Everything is moving, yet we usually see reality as stationary or solid. When we look at pictures of sacred geometry, we see them as two or three dimensional on a piece of paper or artwork. In actuality, these sacred geometry patterns are moving all over our reality and are the geometric aspects of living light.

They are currents and angles of light. We call these the platonic forms, which are the tetrahedrons, cubes, octahedrons, dodecahedrons, and icosahedrons, turning into our realities that we live in. All five platonic forms have the chestahedron in it and according to Frank Chester, you can say that "all the platonic forms are unified by the way they relate to the archetype of the seven-sided form," also known as the chestahedron. This is interesting as the number seven is known by the Arcturians to be the transmutation back to light.

Back to the oneness!

If a tetrahedron is aligned correctly on a geometric position with harmonic interaction with light (or the star of a system), it will channel cosmic energy because of the four forces of the universe or the unified field. This is what the great pyramid of Giza is doing when it aligns with the star of Sirius. I see these geometric patterns sometimes with my physical eyes or third eye. They are beautiful and sometimes they look like a kaleidoscope moving in many different patterns. If you spin around and around, then stop and close your eyes, you can see some of these patterns.

These forms move throughout the cosmos in toroidal fields (like our body auras, volcanos, and blackholes), counter-rotating gyres (like the way a figure eight moves), linear motions (the way a river moves with some water moving in the other direction), and more. Regardless, balance is always maintained.

There is just so much out there that we don't usually see with our physical eyes, yet it still exists.

I am fascinated with the language of energy and I have much to learn as much has been lost. Our English language is like speaking spells to each other and leaves much to be desired. The language of energy is with words and creates our material world.

There is also light language that carries unconditional love, divine creativity, and infinite knowing as well as it being alive and conscious. According to the Arcturians in the book, *The Journey Continues: The Arcturian Corridor Part II,* "Light language is a component of multidimensional light that flows from the ONE and is the form of communication for all multidimensional beings." It resonates beyond space and time. Light language is the motion that moves in and out, weaving the language of energy. It stirs and shapes the energy of the cosmos making all types of shapes, having layers upon layers of information.

The Hawaiian language is a seed language and is powerful in creating what you want especially through chants and the hula, which is like light language. Ancient Polynesians knew how to put energy in or out of something with the hula just as Tai Chi works in the same way. In the book, *Change We Must* by Nana Veary, she talks about how the ancient chants were in idioms and how the ancient Hawaiian language was in metaphor that sounded like poetry. It was a melodious and graceful language, but was lost when the missionaries converted their language into the written word.

Nana Veary said, "'Alo'" means the bosom, the center of the universe. 'Ha' is the breath of God. The word is imbued with a great deal of power. I do not use the word casually. Aloha is a feeling, a recognition of the divine. It is not just a word or greeting." Most of us don't realize the power of this word and the depth of the meaning.

The ancient Hawaiians were taught to speak their language softly and to leave out the details. Nana Veary's mother practiced silence, the secret power of the kahunaism, as silence allows you to go to the source of your being…"the still, all-knowing center." Nana's mother told her to use her hands and not to talk as you waste your energy talking. This is interesting as the Hawaiians are connected to the Pleiadians and the Arcturians. The advanced ETs don't speak unless they know what they want to create. They don't dissipate their energy with idle chatter and their words carry power when they speak.

We are made of light and some people can see the lights around others. I can see this when I let my eyes look past someone or something. There is light around trees, plants, and rocks…really everything, and it is amazing to see how big auras can be. The more light you have, the healthier you are. As you develop your consciousness, you develop your light. Generate it by bringing in more electricity into your system.

Doug Vogt found that the shapes of plasma energy in various positions as they move through the torus of magnetic energy surrounding the Earth are the symbols of the Hebrew language. It is also some of the symbols on spaceships. Letters, numbers, and sounds are all equivalent and you can create with any of them according to Dan Winter's book, *Fractal Conjugate Space and Time*.

Dreams are their own language and if we understand them, we can understand what our subconscious is trying to tell us. We may be working through something, know what is coming, or have an epiphany. This would help us to be better creators of this world. In dreaming, we can discover other parts of ourselves, meet other beings, go out of the body, and create/integrate new skills.

In *Dreams: Your Magic Mirror* by Elsie Sechrist, she talks about how dreams teach us how to use the language of energy with intent. This is how our reality is created. We are creating other worlds in our dreams as the nature of consciousness is to create. Dreams are not lesser realities, but your multidimensional self creating in other worlds. It's all just a dream!

Mathematics is also a language of energy as calculus is really about truth, algebra is about balance, and adding/subtracting is all about creating more or less. Every single formula is a set of numerical descriptions of some kind of movement or transaction between various entities that exist in space. They are all frequency formulas and numbers are alive!

Geometry is the bridge between the "One" and the many (numbers) and is the purest visible expression of a number according to Michael S. Schneider in his book, *A Beginner's Guide to Constructing the Universe.* The nature of the circle as one, also gives rise to the many as it moves from a single circle to the vesica piscis to the seed of life to the flower of life and beyond, creating form. Michael Schneider said, "Numbers, shapes, and their patterns symbolize omnipresent principles, including wholeness, polarity, structure, balance, cycles, rhythm, and harmony."

The language of mathematics was actually the study into natural science and understanding yourself in ancient Greece under Pythagoras. These students were called "matekoi" or "those who studied all." Schneider said in his book, "The word 'mathema' signified 'learning in general' and was the root of the Old English 'mathein,' 'to be aware,' and the Old German 'munthen,' 'to awaken.'"

Most of us hear the word math and either love or hate it, as math felt like memorizing and getting the right answer instead of understanding that numbers and shapes are symbols of principles to teach us about the structure of the universe. The simple counting of numbers from one to ten with the shapes that represent them (like a circle, line, or triangle), express a consistent and comprehensible language according to the ancient mathematical philosophers. These first ten numbers are the original blueprints for designs found throughout our cosmos.

Mathematics could also be considered a philosophical language as numbers and their associated shapes represent the stages in the process of becoming. Each number and shape were personified in ancient cultures representing a certain god or goddess. For example, the goddess Athena was represented by the number seven or seventy-seven as her name added up to in gematria.

We live in a much more fascinating universe than we are taught in school and it is time to take the mystery out of universe by taking another perspective of mathematics and geometry. Plato said, "Numbers are the highest degree of knowledge. It is knowledge itself." Geometry and numbers are the blueprints of the cosmos.

Music is considered a universal language because you can communicate across cultural and linguistic boundaries. You can feel good with the frequency of the music which can put out glorious colors to enhance your wellbeing. Frequencies are what we are all created from and the Solfeggio frequencies are very healing. We could change our world here on Earth if we really brought out harmonically balanced healing frequencies instead of music that plays on our emotions of sadness or anger.

Remember, it is frequency that determines our perception and experience. "All knowledge is already deep within us, so no one can really teach us anything new," according to Plato. We just need to remember the great wisdom of the cosmos and rejoin our Galactic neighbors. So much more to explore!

What if the Galactics want to help us?
What if we need their help?
What if we are coming into big Earth changes?

Are we coming close to experiencing a micronova?
Are we going to experience a grand solar minimum?
Are we going to have massive polar shifts?

Why do many Galactics live inside their planet?
Do you still think humans are the only ones out there with intelligent life?

We as a planet are facing some challenges in the future. Micronovas, the grand solar minimum, and polar shifts can destroy life on Earth as we know it. Planets can be volatile and Earth is one of those. She is alive and to heal herself, all she needs to do is to make a pole shift which would cause land and water to shift in many ways, wiping out continents as we know them today. Water would be where land is and land would be where water is.

A micronova would be a blast from the sun and would destroy anything in its path. So, whatever way the planet is facing, all of that would be destroyed. There would be huge destruction. Maybe that is what happened to Mars or Venus? Is that why they live inside the planet?

We need the Galactics help to either get off the planet and go to a more stable one. Perhaps we could somehow teleport our Earth away while the micronova happens or somehow help the Earth to heal herself before a pole shift?

Maybe we just need a "force field" around the Earth?!

As I mentioned before, we are on the fifth round of humans on this Earth. You can find this information on Gossford Glyphs in Australia which lays out the rise and fall of humans every 12,000 or so years. The Mayans also back this up which is described in a book called *The 8 Calendars of the Maya* by Hunbatz Men. We are the next experiment of humanoid beings on this planet hoping to evolve our planet before the micronova explosion from the sun every 12,068 years or so or a pole shift where the poles move and the Earth rotates the opposite way.

There is also the grand solar minimum which occurs every four hundred years and we are a few years in already. This is where everything gets colder and intermittent freezing happens all year long. The cycle lasts anywhere from thirty to several hundred years. It can cause crops to collapse and famine to occur along with disrupting our global civilization and toppling governments.

There have been discoveries of skeletons of great giants, tiny humanoids, man-beasts with horns and tails, and many others on this planet. Much of this was hidden away as they were being discovered in the early 1900s by the Smithsonian which was owned by those in power. They didn't want us to know of our ET connections or to have it challenge our religions.

Doug Vogt wrote a book called *God's Judgment Day* in 1977, but didn't publish it until 2007 where he describes the micronova and clock cycle (where the solar system renews, regenerates, and re-synchronize themselves). Vogt says that we are at the end of our 12,068 year cycle with the sun and that it is up in 2046 plus or minus 275 years. It is already showing signs of the micronova and it can occur anytime. Our intelligence agencies contacted Vogt and wondered how he figured it out, but Vogt refused to meet because he knew they would confiscate his research.

Doug Vogt, Chan Thomas, and Ben Davidson all concur that a micronova is a "sneeze" from the sun that will blast one side of the Earth with superheated gases destroying everything in its path. Chan Thomas wrote a book called *The Adam and Eve Story* in the 1950s where he had figured out as well. Our intelligence agencies came in and took his book away, classifying it to be top secret. Eventually, they published a sanitized version years later under his name.

Why don't they want us to know what is coming?
Perhaps they already inhabit the inner Earth?
Are they only saving a select few?

Going back to the micronova, the dust cloud would be moving at a rate of 1500 miles per second and then encompass the rest of the Earth on the other side with freezing temperatures of below 200 degrees Fahrenheit. The top 1200 feet of the ocean's water that was displaced would then rain down and flood the Earth for weeks, as it came back into the oceans. This is a 12,068 year cyclical clock cycle and shows where the flood stories have come from in our many religions.

Wanna build an "ark" (spaceship) yet?

As for a pole shift, it would make the land fold over on itself, so Norway could be down by middle Europe. Some lands rise and other lands sink.

Is what happened in Atlantis and Lemuria?

We have choices to work together and evolve our consciousness to heal our Earth which could ease a pole shift. As for the sun, we are approaching the "sneeze" which can happen any time before or after 2046 and some "seers" are seeing some of these changes come in 2027 or 2028 in a more minor way.

We are creating our world with our thoughts and can shift our thinking to positive thinking. Why do we continue to fight with one another when we could be coming together to try to evolve past these disasters? Could we all together form a field of energy around the planet to be untouched by the potential disasters? Could a community do the same thing? Could we do so as an individual and form a column of light around yourself...like a "force field?"

Immanuel Velikovsky, in his book, *Worlds in Collision*, talks about how there will be great destruction, but that there is major and minor versions of destruction because our solar system is dynamic. The sun is already changing from golden to more white and beginning to swell which are signs that it is close. We need to find a way to get off our planet and even out of our solar system. We could go into the inner Earth or face being destroyed. Shifting our consciousness could buy us a few more years to evolve.

The Pleiadians know how to survive and are all about teaching others how to survive especially those who are facing extinction like us with these cyclical events. This is why they are helping us to evolve our consciousness, so that we can evolve and have the ability to get off the planet if we need to. Expanding our consciousness will also evolve our technologies and sciences giving us the ability to build conscious spaceships.

Mother Nature is the physical reality of spirit and not separate from the human spirit. Humanity is of nature and not separate in consciousness. Therefore, human negativity and collective fear is a creative force that expresses in violence and in violent storms. In the book, *Journey into Nature*, Michael is talking with a violent storm which says, "Just as suppressed rage of an individual eventually explodes in temper, so also the accumulated fears, spites, and hates of humanity unleash all the forces of a tempest." So, many storms of destruction that rage are really the reflected storms of rage within the human psyche.

Pan, the god of the inner realm and Mother Nature, says from *Journey into Nature*, "More subtle by far, yet no less powerful is the effect of negative thinking in the natural world. Nature is affected by negative action and negative thoughts. Seldom do humans realize this. Very rarely do humans even consider the possibility that the quality of their thoughts might affect Nature."

This says it all.
Are we ready to come together?
We need to work together.
Let's evolve our consciousness!
I know we can do this!

Are you ready to be powerful?
Not power over others, but power with others?
Are you afraid of your power?
If so, why is that?
Are you a victim?

Do you have memories of abusing your power in other lifetimes?

What if you already are powerful, but you have just forgotten?

To join the Galactic community, we need to be in our power. We need to have expanded our consciousness and be able to have broader abilities like telepathy and clairvoyance. Just decide to take one step in this direction and the universe will meet you there.

What does "stepping into our power" mean? It means that we are not in fear. Power is the ability to decide and do. It is also the willingness to create knowingly and on purpose. We are incredibly powerful, but we have been taught that we are not.

Humans have not given ourselves permission to be powerful and to develop our power. We don't have any inner authority to do what we think is best. Are you ready to give your inner authority permission to develop your power?

It is important to note that this does not mean power over others and abusing your power. Some of us may be afraid of our power and remember lifetimes where we did abuse our power. It is time to heal those lifetimes and get rid of the old fear program which has been keeping us stuck.

Every thought creates and we are creating our realities around us haphazardly. Learn to control your thoughts and to let those go that are from fear and doubt. Focus only on what you want to see in your reality. Practice mindfulness. Thoughts are like a pebble that is dropped into a glass of water. As the ripples go out, they hit the edge of the glass and come back in. They come back to you in physical form as if you were the pebble whether you are creating consciously or not.

We are taught to sleep, eat, go to school/work, be entertained, and to not question the deeper parts of our world. We are taught that religion has the answers and just to believe. Instead, we need to go within.

To step into your power is to "Know Thyself." First, develop your sense of humor. Laugh and laugh a lot. Be funny as it raises your vibration. You will transform your consciousness which is really just changing your frequencies. You have done the deeper inner work to understand and heal your traumas. You have re-imagined old traumas, molding them the way you want them as all of reality is malleable...nothing is set in stone. The more energy you put into the new scene or being, the quicker you can become it.

You have had your "judgment day" which is really the day you stopped judging yourself and others. You see the absurdity of the human condition with all the fighting and duality. You see a bigger picture. You are falling in love with yourself and everything. You are open, exploring Mother Nature by being in it and telepathing with all in Mother Nature.

You realize everything has a consciousness and humans are not the only intelligence because everything is intelligent. You are exploring your past and future lives and gaining the teachings from them. You are remembering your connections to other worlds and reality systems. You are remembering your mission and reason for being here now.

You know who you are!

There are many spiritual teachers like Eckart Tolle and Jane Roberts in her *Seth* books that say, "The point of power is in the present" or that our power comes from the "Now." All of Source is ready and waiting at your fingertips when you are present every moment, living without fear.

We all start somewhere. Let's move gently, fiercely, and fully into consciousness. No judgment! It takes time, practice, and integration along with patience, humility, and a spirit of adventure. When you begin to "feel" a shift, your frequencies are changing.

Here are some ideas to begin stepping into your power and expand your consciousness:

+Let the universe know you want to expand your consciousness. You are ready.

+Become an observer instead of a reactor and suspend judgment. Practice feeling and not thinking. Recognize when the energy changes around you.

+If old fears or angers arise, feel them and allow them to dissipate instead of not dealing with them as they will continue to haunt you if you don't. Look them in the face and you will see them turn from a lion into a kitty cat. Practice the law of stillness.

+Practice remembering your dreams and learn what they mean. They are a preview of what's to come.

+Practice really listening as if for the first time. Practice really seeing for the first time. Look and listen with the ears and eyes of a child.

+Practice opening your heart to someone or something. Allow this to change you.

+Connect to the God/Goddess (I AM) within and allow it to merge with you. Develop a relationship as it wants to know itself through you. This is how you connect to your power within.

+Do things in meditation like cooking, dancing, drawing, gardening, carpentry, or writing. Try fasting to see what happens to your consciousness when not digesting food.

+Develop your telepathy by practicing communicating with Mother Nature as everything is alive and communicates. Develop a relationship with all parts of it including the elements, animals, insects, plants, trees, rocks, fairies, divas, elves, etc...

+Practice holding the intent of what you want and moving in a symbolic way through dance, chanting, breathwork, etc...

+Try to hold the realization in your mind that everything you can see around you, is you. Nothing is not you and nothing is separate from you. It is you in different forms just in another disguise, but still you!

We are incredibly powerful, but we just don't practice. Just pick one or two of these and play with them. Have fun with them.

Also, when we are in an altered state, we can move energy quickly. If you see a situation ask, "What good can I do?" Be quiet and listen. Whatever you do will show up in the physical as that energy is in this reality. This also works quickly when you become lucid in a dream.

As I mentioned before, one thing that I like to do is to merge with Source by letting my field become permeable. I merge my energy with the "I AM" around me and expand into the power of everything. Play with this and be curious. Merge with your car as a spaceship and become conscious with your car. This is part of learning about conscious spaceships. You can even fix your car this way!

Remember, we need to develop our power or those who have a more expanded consciousness can violate our will. You came here to step into your personal power. We must attend to our power and consciousness! Go within and connect to "the Force" (the God within) as the advanced ETs do. Develop yourself and give your inner authority permission to be powerful.

To step into your power is to bring yourself back to finding the God (Source) within yourself. We are taught to look outside ourselves instead of finding everything we need within ourselves. Jesus, Buddha, Moses, and many other masters all taught the same thing, but we tend to put them on pedestals thinking we can't do what they do.

It is just the contrary, we can do what they do and more (which is what Jesus said). The true meaning of Christ or Buddha Consciousness is connecting to the God (Source) within yourself. This is the meaning of the second coming of Christ…as we will be one with the God/Goddess within. Christ was actually a title meaning "Illuminated One."

You are the Christ.
You are the Buddha.
It is a state of consciousness.
May "the Force" be with you.

How are you feeling after reading all this?
Does any of it resonate?
Is there a part of you that feels truth?

Did you come from the stars?
Are you Intergalactic Intelligence?

Is your head buzzing?
Are you excited or freaking out?!

Are you ready to expand your consciousness more?
Perhaps you already connect with your ET family?
Maybe you remember your true mission on Earth?

There is lots of information here in this book that is not "mainstream," yet it may or may not resonate with you. Feel into what is true for you and ask to remember your true origins. This information may blow up your beliefs and the foundation of your reality. It may leave you wondering who you really are. There is part of you that is ready for this or you would not have attracted this book into your life.

You may have had new insights and be integrating this information for some time. It may expand your view of this reality system and what your experience on Earth is really all about. There is an old matrix on Earth that has been here to keep us distracted and to keep us from expanding our consciousness. Once we break free of the matrix and let go of old beliefs, so much opens up!

We can fly!

We are the blend from the dust of the Earth and the cosmic stuff of the Star beings. We have the seeds of ETs within us and this is what is ready to be awakened now. Our consciousness is connected to many other advanced civilizations. The secret of life is maintaining communication and unity with the universe.

We are electric beings within an electromagnetic universe of light. Electricity triggers the birth of galaxies, stars, and planets. Will we humans one day search the skies for the truth of our origins?

Can you imagine if we had 8 billion of us on planet Earth coming together in unity and focusing our consciousness for good? It actually doesn't take a whole lot of us to transform a population and there is a huge power here. The current powers in charge do not want us to realize how powerful we are together and would like to reduce the population because of this fact.

From the words of Abraham-Hicks, "One person in alignment with Source is more powerful than one million who are not."

We are that powerful.

Love is the most powerful force in the universe. We need to learn how to use this and embody this. We have so much help out there and the Galactic civilizations are looking to connect with you.

Are you ready?

We are not alone, nor have we ever been.

Are you ready to wake up?

Remember?

It's time!

We got this!

You are loved and cherished on every dimension. The names and numbers do not matter. They do not mean anything to you. What is meaningful to you is your own heart, your own soul, your own consciousness, your own potential, your own divine beauty. However, we desire you to know you are not alone.

~P' TAAH (Pleiadian)
From the book *P' TAAH, The Gift* by Jani King

Resources

Jean-Luc Bozzoli: www.eyewithin.com

Frank Chester: www.frankchester.com

Dr. Thomas Cowan: www.faim.org/dr-thomas-cowan

Lisa Denning: www.lisadenning.com
www.etsy.com/shop/LisaDenningImages

Abraham-Hicks: www.abraham-hicks.com

Penny Kelly: www.consciousnessonfire.com
www.patreon.com/pennykelly and on YouTube

Tom Kenyon: www.tomkenyon.com

Keshe Foundation: www.keshefoundation.org
www.kfssi.org

Elizabeth Klarer: *Beyond the Light Barrier* and YouTube

Dr. Susanne Lie: www.multidimensions.com

Barbara Marciniak: www.pleiadians.com

Dr. Norma Milanovich: www.ourtrustisingod.com

Joan Ocean: www.joanocean.com
www.etfriends.com

Plasma Info: www.safireproject.com or www.aureon.ca

Dr. Gerald Pollack: www.pollacklab.org

Rob Potter: www.thepromiserevealeduat.com

Dr. Jerry Tennant: www.tennantinstitute.com

Elaine Thompson: www.elaine-thompson.com

About the Author

Hydee Tehana has a deep love for the Galactics and the cosmos remembering some of her lives within different advanced ET civilizations. She knows that she is acting as a Galactic Ambassador here to help shift the paradigms in helping humans remember their place in the Galactic family. Hydee thrives on her deep loving relationship with the "I AM."

She loves adventure and travel along with swimming in the ocean with her ocean friends as much as possible. Time travel, space travel, and teleportation are close to her heart as well as being deeply connected with all of Mother Nature.

Hydee was a Captain/paramedic in the fire department for just over twenty years. She also has her master's degree in psychology and is a licensed psychotherapist. Hydee is currently working on evolving consciousness on this planet through speaking, teaching, authoring books, producing enlightened movies, and most importantly, expanding her own consciousness.

She is really just a big kid in an adult body who sometimes acts her age while exploring this amazing universe. Her favorite age to be is eight because eight reminds her of being playful and full of wonder. She remembers the greater meaning of life and what it was like on the other side while taking on a human incarnation this lifetime. Life is meant to be fun and to follow our joy!

To contact Hydee Tehana:
hydeetehana.com

What If